Mothers at Work

How Real Women
Successfully Combine
a Career and Family

A Portrait of Working Mothers in the 1990s

MELANIE HART

Michael O'Mara Books Limited
in association with SHE MAGAZINE

First published in 1997 by
Michael O'Mara Books Limited
9 Lion Yard, Tremadoc Road
London SW4 7NQ

ISBN 1-85479-694-1

A CIP catalogue record for this book
is available from the British Library

Designed and typeset by Martin Bristow

Printed and bound in England by Cox & Wyman, Reading

For my darling Natalie

——

With thanks to Paulene for all her help

Contents

Introduction

'You look nice Mummy,' my two-year-old daughter said, looking me up and down appreciatively through bleary, fist-rubbed eyes. 'You're going to work today, aren't you?'

'Yes, darling, and you're going to see Lorraine,' I replied, keeping the tone light, while mentally calculating that I had half an hour to get Natalie washed, dressed, breakfasted and out of the door for the twenty-minute pushchair ride to the childminder's house.

'You go to work on train don't you, Mummy, and Daddy goes in car?' she continued, raising her arms for me to pull off her pyjama top.

'That's right.'

'You work at big desk and Daddy works underwater (he's a commercial diver).'

'Uhuh.' Pyjama bottoms off in one yank.

'Mummy, I'll go on train today. I can do your job,' she said airily. 'Daddy's is too dangerous.' Career decision made, she thrust her thumb back in her mouth and lay down to have her nappy changed.

If only we could make career choices as quickly and easily as our children. Most of us agonize about working long hours and missing out on our children's early years, but as one in five UK women are now the main breadwinners and mortgage payers, the chauvinist's taunt of 'a woman's place is in the home' falls as flat as a repossession letter hitting a doormat.

Money is obviously the main motivator for us to leave four- and five-month-olds, often in strange arms, for x-many daylight hours a week, but not the only one.

I loved my maternity leave but can remember feeling a mixture of sadness and anticipation as I packed bottles, nappies and toys into a bag for Natalie's first full day at Lorraine's house. I was, truth be told, quite excited to be leaving behind the constant round of nappy changing, bottle feeding and washing and ironing until the weekend. I longed to return to using the parts of my brain that had lain dormant for four and a half months. Would I still be able to, and how would I cope with all the organization involved in ensuring that both Natalie's and my days went as happily and smoothly as possible every day?

To find out how other women manage to combine their working and home lives; to see if attitudes have changed since 'the career-is-everything' 1980s; and to pick up some useful hints for myself and my friends, I decided to question some 300 working mothers from all around the UK and Eire on every aspect of their lives.

Aged between 21 and 56, and working in a wide range of professions, from company director to student teacher and scientist to florist, all these busy women made time to answer my questions fully. In the following chapters they speak frankly and emotively about their strengths and failings as employees, mothers, lovers, daughters and friends.

They reveal the most intimate details about their partners, sex lives and bank balances; discuss any feelings of guilt and insecurity; and provide a wealth of advice and simple tips – for everything from dealing with emergencies, leaky breasts and unfaithful men, to the best ways to relieve stress and relax our minds and bodies – to make all our lives easier.

Work

'Interesting, challenging, rewarding but tiring!'

If you won the jackpot on the National Lottery, would you give up work in an instant? Me too. No more rushing around, no more deadlines to meet, no more decisions to make and late-night crises. Who am I kidding? I would be doing all this and more – but as a full-time mother instead.

So maybe a compromise would be best. I could set aside a couple of days a week to work on a special project, or buy into a business . . . well, we can all dream, can't we?

More than two thirds of the 300 women who contributed to this book said that, much as they loved their children, they would not like to give up their jobs completely. Nearly half of them went back to work out of financial necessity having had children, but one in three also admitted that they needed the mental stimulation and buzz provided by even an eight-hour-a-week job in order to make them feel valued both in and outside the home.

More than two thirds loved their job and, despite the bad press often received by successful women at the hands of a male-dominated media, nearly half saw themselves as 'career women'. A further 27 per cent said that they were currently treading water until their children were older.

Most of the women to whom I spoke work full time (47 per cent), one third work part time, one in five are lucky enough to be able to spend school holidays with their children – or to have secured good flexitime rotas with their employers – and just three per cent are in job shares.

So, do work colleagues appreciate the amount of skill, dedication and life experience we bring into work with us each day? Apparently not. One third of those questioned said that colleagues often doubted their commitment to their jobs and made life difficult for them; while half weren't sure what their colleagues thought.

How do you feel about your job?

'My work gives me a buzz!'
Ann, 41, chartered accountant

'I don't see myself as so much of a career woman as I did in my 20s and 30s because children have greatly affected my working life. I don't believe you can do both successfully.'
Lesley, 40, photographer/book-keeper

'I feel my job is as dull as ditchwater. I only decided to return to work to pay the mortgage! I could be swimming, walking, playing bridge, having pub lunches, studying, gardening.'
Brenda, 43, office worker

'My plan was to marry and have children while my husband and I were both young, to enable us to enjoy our life together once the children had gone to school and I was able to work again. Unfortunately, when my second son Michael was six years old and our plan was beginning to come together, my husband was killed in a car accident. I work full time now but am trying to reduce my hours, I hope to do four days a week. I grew up expecting to be a wife and mother, never a career woman – although I enjoy it now, I have to admit.'
Jackie, 36, accounts clerk/estate agent

'I enjoy the work, but I hate the office politics that go with it. I just can't be bothered with the pettiness of it – I guess it wasn't so petty when work was my life.'

Janette, 30, senior systems analyst

'I thoroughly enjoy it, but wish there were two of me – one for work and one for my children at home.'

Catherine, 28, branch administrator

'Most of the time it's okay. I prefer it when we are busy and I would like to be promoted, but the university is a good employer. I don't particularly want to get to the top, but I do want to have an enjoyable career.'

Jane, 25, housing officer

'It's nothing like as enjoyable as it was twenty years ago. Between them Parliament and others have made it less so. I'd prefer to work only four days a week now.'

Mary, 46, teacher

'I enjoy it. It's very demanding, but I need to be stretched. I do have to watch out, though, that this doesn't push over into being stressed.'

Jean, 44, senior probation officer

'I feel satisfied, sometimes frustrated, but always committed and enthusiastic. After two years off I panicked about having lost my vocabulary and being left behind the rapid advances being made in medicine. I love to work. I have significant knowledge and skill and while I still feel enthusiastic about working, I will continue. With five children I also need the money. I have a maturity and realism that I lacked before.'

Judith, 36, chartered physiotherapist

'I realize that it gives my life balance, keeps me more alive and gives me more self-respect. It pays the mortgage etc. and keeps both my brain and my marriage alive.'

Julie, 29, accountant

'I find it interesting and challenging and rewarding, but tiring! I couldn't leave nine years of hard work and achievement behind. It gives a feeling of self-worth.'

Helen, 27, business development consultant

'I love my job as a hairdresser. I own my own business, so I had no choice about returning to work. I would be so bored at home with nothing to do except meet other mothers and talk about babies.'

Mandy, 28, hairdresser

'It's a vocation. I'm a good teacher and I find it rewarding and fulfilling. I had stepped right down the promotion ladder but am working back up it again.'

Pauline, 41, teacher

'I'm slightly bored. I've been there 13 years but am afraid to move because of job security; working part time would be less stressful. I have stayed put because I am the only wage earner. Having to think of Jason has made me afraid to risk a change of job.'

Judy, 39, customer service officer

'I enjoy my job; it's interesting, challenging and can be eventful and stressful. I am not a "high-flier" particularly. Children, although very important, are not everything for all time.'

Margaret, 47, senior medical laboratory scientific officer

How has having children affected your working life?

'I don't take work home now, unless it's essential. I started a job share after I had my second child.'

Theresa, 37, teacher

'I was due to start work in London as a retail manager before my daughter was born. When I got pregnant, I could not take the job because of the travelling. It was several years before I got into a reasonable job after that.'

Jane, 25, housing officer

'I like to get as much out of life and everything that I do as I can. I feel more motivated and confident since I have had Martin.'

Sarah, 26, florist/student

'I decided to give up my former job as a viola player, and work from home as a composer. So having children has propelled me into doing what I've always wanted to do.'

Sally, 39, composer

'Having children transformed my working life completely. I resigned from my job and made the decision to go freelance – maybe the push I needed. Work is a vital part of my life; it boosts my confidence and self-esteem.'

Louise, 35, freelance market research moderator

'My working life has not been affected at all. I love training people. It fits in very well and my son really respects the fact that I work – he's better for it.'

Sue, 35, training manager

'I never have time for myself and spend half my time trying to make extra time to spend with my family.'

Karen, 28, caterer

'Previously I was an executive officer in the Health Service and photography was more of a hobby. When I left to have Ian, I decided to start my own wedding photography business so that I could work from home and still be able to take the major responsibility for my children's upbringing.'

Pam, 32, wedding photographer

'I always used to work full time in one job; I do find it better having a few jobs (part time). I can work around my daughter doing care work and my business is only down the road from my house so she calls in on her way from school if I am there all day.'

Joy, 41, general assistant/proprietor of own business/care assistant

'I did not go back to my career until both the children were at school. I took time out to bring up the children. Technology continued to develop, but the children helped me mature as an individual. I am still working in marketing, but I'm sitting formal exams and moving into a management position.'

Lynda, 41, marketing executive

'My priorities have changed and my family would always come first now.'

Sally, 24, library assistant

'I have become self-employed, and now run my own marketing consultancy business from home.'

Claire, 34, marketing consultant

'My job is a way of life. And while the idea of not working is lovely, I'd get bored without the challenge. I have reduced the breeding stock numbers though, because it is hard to devote 365 days a year to animals when you have the responsibility of a child.'

Francesca, 31, horse breeder/business partner

'I work part time – 30 hours a week during term time. I feel it is "beneath me", not at all challenging. I would certainly have progressed far further along my original path if I hadn't had children. I returned to work when they were both at school.'

Yvonne, 38, research assistant (pharmacology)/Techno-Science & IT technician in a school/college

'My working life has changed totally. I used to work mainly in retail shops and now I work in childcare.'

Christine, 34, registered childminder

'Drastically! I know that because I want to spend time with the children, I don't give my business all the time and enthusiasm it deserves.'

Caroline, 32, kennels & cattery proprietor

'Having children has completely transformed me: I used to be a career woman and I have become a female who puts her career firmly second.'

Rona, 28, researcher for Executive Search Agency

'I resent male colleagues who can simply get up and get themselves to work; I often arrive feeling as if I have already done a full day's work.'

Sarah, 37, college lecturer (fashion design)

'Having children has made me a better nurse, because I had a Caesarean and experienced surgery for myself.'

Heather, 31, nurse specialist (infection control)

'When my eldest son was born, I had to take very low-paid work cleaning toilets in a factory, although I was a fully qualified legal secretary. I couldn't afford childcare at that time and it was the only work I could get in the evenings.'

Susan, 45, student/company director

'I think I am a better manager now; I listen to staff and clients and am probably more flexible. Having children also puts problems at work into perspective. I avoid unnecessary travel and make a point of finishing on time. I would rather work through lunch than be late home.'

Lynne, 33, publisher/public relations consultant

'I have become a self-employed contractor so that I can avoid working during school holidays. I also avoid company politics and the pressure to work overtime.'

Maggie, 37, programming consultant

'I have changed the nature of my work. I used to be a dancer on the stage, then before I had Sharon I became a nursery nurse. Then I started my own school. I work next door to home, which is perfect.'

Cherrie, 49, principal of ballet school

Would you prefer not to work?

'Yes. I enjoy my own company, and I can always find plenty to do, like going to the gym, or swimming or doing the housework. I would make better meals and be able to see more of my husband, as he works shifts.'

Susan, 37, WP operator/clerk

'I cannot imagine not wanting to work. I have no desire to climb the promotion ladder but I need to work. It makes me feel more confident and complete. I used to work full time and was always the one to stay late or go in and cover for others. Now I work independently – not as part of a ward – so I've opted out of the management of others. It's bliss!'

Pauline, 31, paediatric endocrine nurse specialist

'I was nearly 40 when I had my baby and I felt that if I gave up work at that stage, I would never get another "proper" job again. I am shy. My job provides most of my social interest. If I gave it up, I would be left more or less with only my home and family and solitary interests such as studying and reading. I was frightened that if I gave up work, I would end up living my life through my child.'

Audrey, 41, admin supervisor

'I enjoyed my job until recently, but now I resent having to work full time. I would rather not work at all (although if I wasn't working at all, I think I would probably change my mind!)'

Lynda, 34, registered nurse

'I didn't have any choice about returning to work: nobody can afford a mortgage on one income after the Thatcher years. I would prefer to work part time on full pay!'

Sharon, 33, design manager

'No, I like the stimulation and financial independence. I returned to work after my husband left for someone else.'

Christine, 42, resource manager (publications)

'Yes, I would prefer not to work; it would be an easier life. And I see one-parent families who live off benefits doing just as well as I do – but without the stresses that I have.'

Maria, 33, accountant

'I work in Tesco's to make ends meet: my husband walked out when Andrew was ten weeks old. He pays no maintenance and has succeeded in stringing the Child Support Agency (CSA) along. I enjoy college, but could do without working part time as well. But I am now looking for a career because I am the sole breadwinner for three kids. I have become career-oriented because of changes in my personal circumstances.

'I realize now that today, because of changing family values, the chances of young women being left to rear a family on their own have considerably increased. If I do nothing else with my life, I will make sure that my two daughters both have careers they can fall back on.'

Kathleen, 36, student teacher/part-time shop assistant

'I would get very bored if I was at home full time. My daughter has cerebral palsy and needs lots of support. Being at work in a jobshare gives me a break.'

Stephanie, 30, targeting analyst

'No, I work part time (25 hours per week) and find it demanding and enjoyable. I decided to return to work for money and to keep my skills up to date. I need stimulation and adult company and it encourages the children to help at home.'

Jean, 44, doctors' receptionist/typist

'*I prefer to work. I love my independence. The children will move away, and I still want to be Sarah and not just a wife and mother when that happens.*'
Sarah, 25, manager of retail/mail-order leisurewear company

'*To me, not working would be a waste of my education; I have a first-class Honours BSc from university.*'
Wendy, 30, senior computer analyst

'*No. I like to have money to spend as I please. I thought I would be a stay-at-home housewife and look after the children but it wasn't for me.*'
Lindsey, 38, school secretary

'*I would prefer not to have to do the nursing as well as my degree, but we need the money. And it's also an insurance policy for the future, because I'll be able to return to it full time if necessary. I don't want to give up my English degree, if I can avoid it. It's not just to get a better job in the future, it's for me: to prove to myself that I can do it.*'
Helen, 32, staff nurse/full-time student

'*Yes, because I feel I am missing out on a fully satisfying mothering experience. I miss my children.*'
Sarah, 44, social worker/counsellor

'*Yes, I'd rather be at home with Tom while he's young; he's only two years old.*'
Carol, 43, self-employed business administrator

'*No, I felt my horizons were too cramped. And I hated having no money of my own: a present to my husband was really a present to himself.*'
Lindsay, 39, supply teacher (former WRAF personnel officer)

'I couldn't imagine being at home all day with just my partner's salary to live on.'

Anita, 35, software engineer

'I never really considered not going back, because my husband was a student and our financial situation would not have allowed me to give up. Anyway, I enjoy my job and feel I am a person who needs a life outside the home.'

Jill, 39, university administrator

If you have more than one child, did you find it harder to return to work the second time?

'Yes. I was quite ill when I went back 10 weeks after the birth, and with an elder child it was difficult to fit everything in. I just cannot work the 18-hour days I did before. I now do around 10.'

Tina, 37, civil servant

'I found it harder to go back the second time, as there are not the same crèche facilities as there were in Brussels, where I was working when my first child was born. I have changed the nature of my work. I took up photography to enable me to work on Saturday afternoons when my husband could "babysit".'

Lesley, 40, photographer/book-keeper

'I have four children. I eventually returned to part-time work after each child. And in some ways it is easier to return to work, because childcare is the most difficult job of all.'

Claire, 36, social worker

'I did not return to work after my second daughter was born because I did not feel ready to take up my career again. Instead I had a four-and-a-half-year career break, until my third daughter was a year old. I hold a much more responsible position now.'

Sarah, 36, research scientist

'I went back more quickly after my second child. I changed jobs twice during my second pregnancy – for promotion – and I had only been in the third job two weeks when she arrived. Going back was therefore easier. The job I have now just grows and grows.'

Brenda, 33, business development manager

'Yes, it was harder the second time. My children are one and two, born 11 months apart. Leaving my seven-month-old daughter and 18-month-old son was hard because I'd seen more of my son during my second maternity leave, so I knew what I would be missing.'

Catherine, 28, branch administrator

'I only went back to work the second time because of a divorce. But it was harder the first time because my baby was only three weeks old!'

Lucy, 38, secretary/personal assitant & research interviewer

'I found it harder to go back the second time. I have just gone back and it was more of a pull this time because I really enjoy motherhood now and know its rewards.'

Janet, 35, veterinary surgeon

'No, it was easier to go back the second time because I'd been there before; I knew what to expect, and how I would feel.'

Joanne, 26, personnel assistant

'It was harder in the beginning, when one was at nursery and the other at school. It was difficult running to two places in the morning, and I needed help collecting them.'

Wendy, 36, beauty therapist

'It was easier, in fact, the second time. I was more confident as a mother, less worried. My in-laws were living with us then. They are our childminders, so it was the least disruptive arrangement for the children. By the time I had my second child my career was starting to take off, so the "call" from work was clearer.'

Karen, 35, psychologist

Do you work from home? If so, what are the advantages and disadvantages?

'Yes. Before I worked purely to earn money by cleaning, painting etc., but I now enjoy writing immensely and intend to continue. There are many advantages to working from home: I'm comfortable, there are fewer distractions and it's possible to fit my work around my kids. I can't think of any disadvantages.'

Deborah, 36, freelance writer/journalist

'Yes, partly. The advantages are that I can work and look after Charlotte. The disadvantage is that I tend to keep working until at least 11 o'clock each night.'

Karen, 28, caterer

'The problem is that friends think you can chat but domestic chores beckon!'

Nikki, 34, TV producer/journalist

'Yes, I work from home as a florist. I enjoy my job very much, I find it relaxing and very therapeutic. I can be artistic and creative and look forward to a financial reward.'

Sarah, 26, florist/student

'I teach piano after school and the advantage of that is the minimal outlay and that I have no childminding to worry about.'

Lynne, 33, student

'The obvious advantage is being able to fit my work around school and any other commitments the children may have. The only day of the week my job has priority is Saturday, when the weddings take place. The major disadvantage is always being at home and never quite being able to be on my own to concentrate on work – even when my husband is at home and I'm tucked away in the office upstairs. The boys understand and leave me alone, but Emma is only two and often finds her way up to the office.'

Pam, 32, wedding photographer

'Advantages: Very flexible; can work easily in the evenings; no time wasted commuting. Disadvantages: difficult to switch off; sometimes does not present the wholly professional front to clients that I would like.'

Arabella, 33, interior designer

'The advantage is being totally in charge of my children. The disadvantage is that I do not meet other adults.'

Christine, 34, registered childminder

Have you ever felt that colleagues doubt your commitment to your job?

'No. As I work for working parents, they are very understanding. Bethany was once kept in hospital, and my employer couldn't sleep for worrying about her.'

Tracey, 27, nanny/nursery nurse

'I needed to change my work hours from 9 am – 5.30 pm to 8 am – 4.30 pm in order to be able to collect my daughter by 6 pm. When people constantly see you leave "one hour early", they simply do not believe you have a strong commitment to the job. This has created more stress in my life; it has taken two years to learn how to relax again.'

Jane, 35, public relations/marketing manager

'Working part time in the past, there was one female colleague from whom I encountered prejudice. She continually jibed at me going home early, saying "Half day again!"'

Lynda, 41, marketing executive

'Yes, I took a decision on my return; I wanted to be office-based, not available for travel to meetings/conferences etc. This definitely affected my manager's perception of my commitment.'

Mary, 56, customer services manager

'Men are more understanding. Jealous women seize any opportunity to moan.'

Maria, 33, accountant

'Yes. Older female colleagues don't think you should return to work until the kids are at school.'

Julie, 33, secretary

'Recently, I have had to take a great deal of time off because of illness in the family, but on each occasion I have said that I will make up the hours, keep up to date with the work, and take work home, if necessary, and this has been completely acceptable to my employers. They have families too!'

Joanna, 37, local government officer

'No, because I have worked with women who use their children as an excuse for lack of commitment, and I don't do that. But I have also worked with a man who used his hayfever as an excuse to stay at home to watch Wimbledon. Quite simply, women aren't any better or any worse than men!'

Win, 45, speech & language therapist/housekeeper

'My son was in hospital several times with a condition that was worrying and, although I got paid the first couple of times, after that I didn't. Strangely enough, it was my male (childless) manager who was the most supportive throughout.'

Lynne, 33, student

'I've never felt that any of my colleagues have doubted my commitment to my job, but that's probably because I'm the boss and everyone knows that I put more into my work than everyone else. I work more hours; and I take everyone else's unsolvable problems and deal with them quickly and efficiently.'

Sheila, 33, director/company secretary/manufacturer of communication equipment for people who cannot speak

'Yes, I do. Just recently I was recovering from 'flu and the personnel manager had the cheek to ask whether I felt working four hours a day was worthwhile and if it was not too much of a strain. I mean, work is a rest compared to being a full-time mum!'

Michele, 31, secretary

'My ex-boss (female, single, childless, ruthless) used to doubt my commmitment, but my new boss who is male and a family man doesn't seem to!'

Sharon, 33, design manager

'Before I even went on maternity leave, my female boss used to stop me going on courses because "the body of knowledge will be lost to the ward", despite my assurances that I would be returning to work.'

Isobel, 31, psychiatric ward sister

'Not really. I work in a female-dominated area, and many of them have young children, so on the odd occasion that I have had to leave work to go to my daughter, I have had only sympathy and understanding.'

Stephanie, 31, midwife

'When I was pregnant with my first child and told my boss that I intended to return to work after the three months of paid maternity leave, while my husband, who worked at the same workplace, would be applying for a five-year career break in order to look after the baby, my boss told me that once the baby was born I would not want to go back. He also informed me that juvenile delinquents were the products of families where the mother worked, and that if I did go back to work, it would be better to employ a nanny to look after the baby, than to leave my husband in charge. He then told my husband that I would lose all interest in him once the baby was born.'

Rebecca, 30, district forester

'I believe it is hard to be as committed to your job after you have had children; they need to come first. I doubt my commitment more than my colleagues do.'

Jacqueline, 29, personnel officer/personal assistant

'I don't in my current job, but I was made redundant within six months of returning to work after my first child. When I was pregnant one of my managers actually said that I would be better off as a librarian!'

Mary, 34, business analyst (IT)

'No – quite the opposite, in fact; they doubt my commitment to my child because I haven't taken the part-time option.'

Julie, 31, careers adviser

'To fit in with my childminder, I start work early (between 7 am and 7.30 am) and finish at 4 pm. I have had several comments from colleagues along the lines of "I tried to get hold of you yesterday, but you had already gone" or "I never seem to be able to catch you these days".'

Christine, 30, financial controller

'No, my boss is extremely supportive. He knows that I will make up any lost time, in the evening or at weekends and he has provided me with a complete electronic office at home.'

Brenda, 33, business development manager

'I used to work for an all-male estate agents' office and I was never allowed time off when my child was ill. My boss even asked me: "Who is more important to you – us or your child?" I would have been fired if I'd given the honest answer.'

Jayne, 38, estate agent

'No, I was actually promoted through applying for a post while I was on maternity leave – I was well chuffed!'

Sarah, 28, regional administrative officer

'Yes, I do. Although my recent request to job-share has been agreed, it is universally viewed as a sign that I cannot cope full *time, rather than as a genuine request to reduce my hours because I want to spend more time with my kids.'*

Stella, 35, housing manager

Tips

1. Don't waste time worrying about returning to work or you will spoil several months of maternity leave unnecessarily.

2. It can be helpful to write down all your reasons for working – so that you can remind yourself why you have chosen to go back.

3. Accept that you might feel guilty, or have mixed feelings, but remember that by going back, you are improving your own life and helping financially with that of your family.

4. If you believe in your decision, everyone else will. If you go back to work when your children are babies, they will treat being cared for by an 'extended family' as normal.

5. Try not to think about what you could be doing with your child while you are at work.

6. Keep in touch with work colleagues while you are on maternity leave.

7. Be aware that the person who was doing your job while you were away might not be delighted to see you back.

8. Discuss your return fully with your partner and ensure that he is prepared to give you the help and support you will need.

9. Make sure you are used to leaving your child with

someone else from an early age, so that he knows you will come back, and, at the same time, you can get used to trusting other people to look after him.

10. Practise the proposed routine for a week or two before you return to work properly.

11. Get organized: get a wall planner, make priority lists and stick to them. Share out household tasks, and get things ready the night before.

12. Buy a play pen; it will prove invaluable when you are rushing to get ready for work, and if you introduce it early enough, your baby will not feel imprisoned.

13. Try to acquire as many labour-saving devices as possible – tumble dryer, dishwasher etc.

14. If at all possible, try to negotiate a flexi-time deal with your boss before you leave to have the baby.

15. If you have had a long career gap before you return to work, try to do a night school course to update your skills; it will increase your confidence too.

16. Don't be intimidated because you've been out of the job scene for a while. Be positive.

17. Make sure that your colleagues know what your constraints are going to be well in advance: 'I have to leave by 5.30 pm to pick up my child at 6 pm', for example.

18. Ensure that you have a contingency plan in place for when you need to work late.

If you are working from home

1. You need to be happy with your own company.

2. Try to devote an area or room just to work, not a bedroom or dining room.

3. Be realistic about the amount of work you can take on. If you don't have time to do something, say so.

4. If you have an idea about something that you feel

you can do from home, don't just think about it, get the ball rolling: do some market research and see if the idea is viable.

5. Allow yourself some time off between 3 pm and 7 pm. You can, if necessary, carry on working when the children are in bed.

6. Find yourself a childminder/nursery and use one or the other on your busiest days, just as if you were going out to work.

Children

'She's been heard to boast to friends about mummy's job'

'Mummy, why do you work so hard?' Natalie asked, little hand in mine as she lay in bed after giving me a welcome-home hug. *'You were very late today.'*
'Yes, I'm sorry I'm home so late, darling.' I said, heart aching at the sight of her big, blue eyes struggling to stay open so that we could chat for a while longer. *'I've been staying late this week so that I can finish all my work before our holiday next week; so that we can be together without interruptions and go to Chessington and all your favourite places.'*

'Wow! Really, Mummy? Chessington World is wonderful. They have Dumbo ride and clowns . . .' she tailed off, sleep pulling her away from me. As I slowly tiptoed backwards out of her room, one eye opened. *'You can go to work, it's okay.'* she whispered, before finally losing the battle against sleep.

Natalie is now two and a half, and so interesting and full of questions that it would have been awful to have to leave her for the first time at this age to return to work. She would have regarded it as a betrayal now whereas, because she has been used to our routine since the age of four and a half months, she knows that it is normal for her to have a different day to me. Anyway, her day is often far more fun than mine so there is plenty to catch up on when we are together.

If many of your friends and relations have young children, you will often find yourself bombarded with advice on when is the best time to return to work.

'Go back before they're six months old.' some urge, 'because they're not too clingy then, and as long as they're loved, changed and fed, they will not notice that you've gone.'

'No, between a year and 18 months is better.' others caution, 'because they're more independent by then and anyway, you've been there for their first crawl, steps and sentences.'

'No, once they're four to five years old and have started school is the best time,' a few maintain, 'because you've seen them through their formative years and you can concentrate on your work knowing that they're happily occupied.'

More than half of the women I surveyed went back to work before their babies were six months old; with just three per cent returning when their children were 18 months old and two per cent when their children were four years old.

So, how do our children benefit from being deprived of our company for up to 40 hours a week? One in three mothers say that they love all the extra things that we are able to buy them and the holidays we can now afford to go on. More than a quarter say their children are more independent and outgoing as a result of mixing with other people and other children before they start school; and 17 per cent admitted that they knew themselves to be happier working and that this must rub off on their children, and must positively affect their relationship with them.

How much maternity leave did you take?

'I had intended to return to work when my first child was six months old, but decided to childmind for friends instead. Eventually I went back to work – and that was evenings only – when the children were four and a half and three. I went back to daytime work when they were six and four and three-quarters.

'I found, much to my surprise, that despite the fact that I thought I would, I just didn't want to work after the first one. By the time they were older, I found that I had had enough of being a full-time mum and wanted a change.'

Valerie, 33, part-time special needs assistant

'I worked until the day before giving birth and returned when he was eight weeks old. I was glad to be back – although I wasn't looking forward to combining housework and work again.'

Mandy, 28, hairdresser

'I took five weeks' maternity leave: four were paid as holiday, one was unpaid (because I'm self-employed). Bethany was three weeks old when I returned.'

Tracey, 27, nanny/nursey nurse

'I was made redundant after my maternity leave (not because of it) but got a new job when Anna was 14 months old.'

Sarah, 31, training manager

'My son was six weeks old when I went back and I took him to the office with me. I was exhilarated at being back in the real world – doing grown-up things – hoping the boss wouldn't walk into the office while I was changing my son's nappy!'

Angela, 35, buyer (for a charity)

'I had six weeks' maternity leave and then I resigned. I continued to do some work in order to "keep my hand in", but the arrangement was flexible and not permanent. I then took a part-time job, then a short-term full-time one, and then, when the children were eight and six years old, a full-time permanent one.'

Pauline, 41, teacher

'I finished work the day I went into labour and returned six weeks later, having had a Caesarian. I was extremely tired and stressed out, but I was able to take Charlotte with me and feed her etc. during breaks.'

Karen, 28, caterer

'I took six months' maternity leave, returning when he was five months old. I had nightmares for a week before returning to work; it was dreadful. I was shunted into a poor-quality job – but at the same rate of pay as before.'

Jill, 34, university technician/owner of a security business

'I didn't have any maternity leave! I gave birth to my second son four hours after I had finished teaching my evening class.'

Myra, 36, TEFL teacher

'My children are both adopted, so I did not qualify automatically for leave; I had to "fight" for it. One of the younger partners in the practice supported my negotiation. The other one's attitude ran along the lines of "pregnancy is an illness, and you're not ill, so you do not need time to recover."'

Christine, 37, general practitioner

'I worked up until three days after my baby was due! Then I took six months' maternity leave from that day. I went back part time for one year, then returned full time. Colleagues welcomed me back because I had made history by being the first probation officer where I live to combine work with a family (baby).'

Charlotte, 50, probation officer

'I was writing an article when my labour started. I finished it and took on another when Will was one week old, but whereas it had been no problem during the pregnancy, it was very stressful after the birth.'

Penny, 39, freelance journalist/editor

'I was in the enviable position of not requiring maternity leave; I simply took special "adoption leave" for eight weeks when the children arrived, and I was able to go part time on a flexi-time basis. Both children (natural brother and sister) were adopted together. I continued on the same pay structure at the same grade as I had been on before.'

Dianne, 40, civil servant

'I had Sara by Caesarian section on the Saturday. My boss had some work that desperately needed doing, so she very kindly brought it into the hospital on the Thursday!'

Julie, 35, hand embroiderer

How did you feel on your first day back at work?

'I felt as if I'd had a limb amputated. I cried all the way to work. Most colleagues tried to understand and other mothers were sympathetic.'

Sharon, 33, design manager

'I felt as though I'd returned from Planet Zonk – relieved to be my own woman again. But I couldn't wait to collect Thomas at the end of the day.'

Gillian, 35, systems training designer

'Colleagues were pleased to see me back. It was heaven to have four hours without nappies etc.'

Michele, 31, secretary

'I felt guilty on my first day back at work, but eager to get back "in the swing".'

Carol, 33, police officer

'I felt very insecure but colleagues were very welcoming. But there was one horrible moment during my first week back after my first baby: I was stuck in a meeting and my breasts started to leak; I just wanted to die of embarrassment. I had to flee to the loo, express some milk and then wear a jacket for the rest of the day, even though it was sweltering hot.'

Sarah, 37, college lecturer (fashion design)

'On my first day back in the salon a colleague asked how old I was. When I replied "30", she said that her mum was 36 and I felt ancient!'

Wendy, 36, beauty therapist

'I felt awful because one of my colleagues wanted my job for her sister and so resented my return.'

Louise, 33, book-keeper

'I felt nervous and fairly stupid because there had been advances made, like the fax and word processing during the time I had been away.'

Evelyn, 34, business information officer

'I was pleased to be back and spent the day checking out changes in techniques that had occurred in my absence. Colleagues were pleased to see me – not so much work for them!'

Margaret, 47, senior medical laboratory scientific officer

'I felt deflated. I would rather have been at home.'

Caroline, 35, manager of a take-away

'I cried all the way to work and felt very shy about going back in. My colleagues did help, especially as I had to express my milk, because my daughter was still fully breastfed. I had to find a dark storeroom to do it in. This brought different reactions ranging from "Why go to such trouble?" to disgust.'

Patricia, 39, operating theatre sister (RGN)

'I was elated to be back in the world of commerce, but felt decidedly guilty about leaving my baby.'

Lesley, 40, photographer/book-keeper

'I felt like a fish out of water on my first day back, totally out of routine. Some colleagues welcomed me; others were quite indifferent.'

Claire, 34, marketing consultant

'I felt very nervous, and worried that I'd forgotten how to do my job. Colleagues were very nice and welcoming.'

Pauline, 31, paediatric endocrine nurse specialist

'I felt like a stranger, because many of the staff had changed during my leave. It was hard getting my brain back into gear.'

Di, 30, quality control supervisor (food industry)

'I was very nervous, but once I was in the office it felt as if I'd never been away. I thought about Elizabeth during the day but *never worried about her. My colleagues were brilliant. I spent all day like a bit of a celebrity – chatting, talking about Elizabeth and catching up on the news.'*

Kathryn, 32, senior computer programmer/analyst

'I felt very inadequate and frightened, in case, as head of the team (ward sister), I had forgotten how to deal with an emergency.'

Heather, 31, nurse specialist (infection control)

'My first day back at work was terrible – a real wrench. After that what I found annoying was that people made assumptions about what I would want to do: not going to meetings late in the day because I was a mother now, for example. It may well have been true, but I wanted to make the decisions and not be treated any differently – even though I know they thought they were trying to help me.'

Carole, 36, bank manager

'I felt lonely and found it difficult walking without a pushchair! Colleagues have been supportive.'

Judith, 36, chartered physiotherapist

In what ways do you think your children benefit from you working?

'As Thomas is an only child, I find the fact that he is mixing with other children an advantage. He learns lots of things from the older children, but I have to take the good with the bad on this one!'

Gillian, 35, systems training designer

'They benefit because I am always home when they are.'
Susan, 37, WP operator/clerk

'My children are more independent. They have better social skills (mixing with other children), and perhaps I am more interesting to talk to!'
Toni, 39, NHS senior manager

'When they were younger, they missed me at times, but now appreciate my need to work. They benefit financially but also in more important ways. I have my own life so don't try to live through them. And they see me as an individual and respect the work I do. My experience and knowledge helps them.'
Sylvia, 40, fee earner (solicitor)

'They have lots of friends, do loads of practical things and play games. They also have a nursery school teacher, French teacher and ballet teacher.'
Janine, 37, doctor

'Financially, we can do more. And that's not to mention that they are less shy and have outside perspectives and a different viewpoint.'
Audrey, 41, admin supervisor

'My daughter benefits because I'm a lot happier. And I have a lot more energy when I'm with her than I would have done.'
Stephanie, 30, solicitor

'When I started back, my daughter said: "Oh good, now we're a normal family." The children didn't like it when they had childminders for short periods, and my hours and holidays mean that the job doesn't impinge on them much.'
Win, 45, speech & language therapist/housekeeper

'*Kristina and Thomas understand what "work" is because I work from home and they see my workplace every day.*'
Ann, 41, chartered accountant

'*I feel Rebecca has benefited a great deal; it's me that has missed out on her. She is a well-developed, outgoing and mostly confident child, who relates well to a good mixture of age groups. She has had a wealth of adventures and experiences that she would probably not have had with me. I am sure it has done her no harm to have had a working mum, and she has been heard to boast to friends about mummy's job.*'
Frances, 38, personal assistant

'*Having two "big brothers" to play with is a great advantage, and the childminder does lots of things like painting/sticking etc. with them that I find it hard to find the energy for.*'
Nicola, 29, antique furniture restorer

'*The children have a very good relationship with their father. They can see the wide range of roles women can have, and I hope this will help them when they grow up.*'
Carole, 36, bank manager

'*I can afford holidays which I would not have been able to otherwise. Martin has had the experience of several foreign countries and now has a clear perception of the world.*'
Sarah, 26, florist/student

'*Whenever I am with my son now, I am happy and glad to be near him. When I was around 24 hours a day, it wasn't like that.*'
Janette, 30, senior systems analyst

'They benefit by seeing that mums can do all kinds of things and still have time for them.'

Catherine, 39, senior secretary

What are your children's main complaints?

'They complain that my husband always gives them pizza!'

Deborah, 36, freelance writer/journalist

'They say I get overtired, and moody. My nine-year-old misses me at bedtime and misses her story. She telephones me at the same time every day to talk to me and I blow her a kiss down the telephone.'

Irene, 42, hotelier

'There are only ever complaints when I'm locked in the bathroom printing pictures!'

Karen, 35, video editor/student

'My children say that I don't sit with them enough and help with homework, as I'm often busy.'

Jean, 44, doctors' receptionist/typist

'They complain that Dad is too strict!'

Anne Marie, 31, part-time sales assistant

'Joe's bottom lip drops when I leave for work; Jack is fine because I often take him to playschool or nursery first. Michael does complain about me working in the holidays, but Kenny is now at an age where he sorts himself out. Jack and Joe are far more independent than Kenny and Michael were at the same age. They are also very sociable, and quite happy in a variety of surroundings and I believe this is because I work and am not at their beck and call all the time, and of course they meet many different people at nursery.'

Jackie, 36, accounts clerk/estate agent

'The children don't like me to go to work in the evenings because I'm not there to put them to bed.'

Helen, 32, staff nurse/full-time student

'I'll use my daughter's quote: "You're the mummy – mummies are supposed to stay at home with their babies."'

Angela, 37, services manager

'The children complain that I am not there to cook lunch.'

Andrea, 43, speech & language therapist/language teacher

'They complain that I never have time to keep the house sparkling but always have time for extra school work.'

Jenny, 50, caretaker/domestic engineer

'The children don't mind me working, but they do complain about me studying.'

Genevieve, 39, NHS administrator

'They complain about not being able to go to friends' houses after school.'

Linda, 37, sales manager

'Occasionally, they feel that I show more concern for my clients than for them.'

Tessa, 42, physiotherapist/aromatherapist

'I have to travel to book fairs in Frankfurt, Italy, Paris and New York about six times a year. The longest that I am away at a time is five days, but my children don't like me going abroad without them. They say: "Why can't Daddy go?"

'Absence does make the heart grow fonder, though, because when I call them and hear their little voices on the telephone, it's so sweet. And I get wonderful welcomes and huge cuddles when I get back. They stick pictures up everywhere and once designed a welcome banner on the computer and hung it up for me.'

Lesley, 41, publisher

'My daughter's complaints range from "Why do you have to work today?" during school holidays, to "All the other mummies can come to —" during term time. If I didn't work, we would be on social security and I would probably be on valium!'

Jane, 25, housing officer

'Molly's only two, but she says she wants me to stay at home with her and play or feed the ducks.'

Sarah, 28, regional administrative officer

Tips

1. Go back to work gradually – part time at first, if you can.

2. Start introducing bottles well before your return so that you will not be having to express too much milk, and so that your baby is happy to be fed by your carer.

3. If you are still breast-feeding before and after work, wear patterned shirts or jumpers and take extra breast pads with you to avoid embarrassing leaks.

4. Take your child to your workplace and show him where you sit etc. so that he knows where you go each day.

5. For both your sakes, get used to being apart from your baby from his earliest days, even if it's just for a few hours a week.

6. Try to have a special time each day: bathtime and bedtime, for example. Plan things for the weekend when the children come first – not the housework.

7. Don't try to overcompensate at work to prove you can cope. But don't use the children as an excuse for arriving late, feeling tired etc.

8. Don't try to overcompensate when you are with the children. They'll still benefit from a healthy balance of love and discipline even when you're not around; they're learning valuable lessons of independence and trust.

9. Buy a mobile phone so that you know you can always be contacted.

10. Remember, if you're happy and confident about your choice of carer, your child should feel the same.

Childcare

'She is safe and I have peace of mind.'

'How can you you leave your baby with a complete stranger?', *'Every child should be with his mother'*, *'If she was mine, I wouldn't let anyone else bring her up – you cannot trust anyone these days.'* Sound familiar? The people who say these sorts of things to mothers who are contemplating returning to work are often those closest to them – even their partners. Who else could wound so effectively, whilst firmly maintaining that they have the new mother's best interests at heart?

If they are willing (a) to pay you to stay at home so that your child doesn't 'suffer', or (b) to volunteer to look after him for you (as long as you'd be happy with them as your carer), then fine; otherwise, you do what is best for you and your family. It is no one else's concern.

More than one third of the women I spoke to chose a childminder as their main carer. Nurseries and relations (not partners) were the second and third most popular options.

Encouragingly, however, more and more husbands/partners are saying "a child should be with his father too" and nine per cent of our sample mothers leave their children with Dad while they go out to work – the same percentage as those who employ nannies. The other options mentioned were au pairs, after-school clubs, mother's helps, friends and workplace creches. The costs ranged from nothing to £220 a week.

The only thing that gave me twinges of guilt about working during Natalie's first couple of years was the fact that I might miss her first crawl, her first proper words and her first steps – the long-awaited early milestones that fill more minutes of video film around the country than all the cringe-making clips in ten series of *You've Been Framed*. But I needn't have worried, because she crawled for the first time one weekend; rolled over on another weekend, obligingly in front of an audience of five just before Sunday lunch at her grandparents' house; and took her first staggering steps around our coffee table one evening. As for talking, she liked the sound of her own voice so much – and still does – that there were plenty of first words to go around.

Children have a certain knack of saving things up to show you. Of course they might get in a bit of practice sneakily when you're not around, a baby dress rehearsal, perhaps, but don't forget to reserve your seat for the command performance, ready with plenty of applause and cuddles to prompt an encore.

Who looks after your child while you are at work?

'We have a live-in nanny, working 50 hours for £70 a week; she was a recommendation from an old nanny. I advertised in the local paper and the standard was appalling: the interviewing was painful. I now have my third nanny this year!'
Julie, 30, business manager

'A nursery looks after my children while I am working: for 32 hours I pay £80 for each (£160 total). One nursery gave my five-month-old son a sandwich. They said it encouraged hand and eye coordination. I removed him and reported them.'
Carol, 33, police officer

'My mother-in-law looks after my boys in the school holidays and for about two hours every day during term time. They love her. It's an ideal arrangement. Mary is family, loving and caring, and she's free!'

Catherine, 39, senior secretary

'A college nursery for 30 hours a week (£36) and my mother, while I work (23 hours – for nothing). The nursery is great; I don't have to worry about the childminder being ill. My mother frequently makes me feel that the children are a burden to her, although I know she wouldn't let me down.'

Kathleen, 36, student teacher/part-time shop assistant

'They are looked after for 10 hours a week. My friends and I swap, so no money is exchanged. It's very erratic at present, and it also means that I have to look after other people's children on other days.'

Deborah, 36, freelance writer/journalist

'I interviewed three nannies, but I wasn't impressed. My greatest worry was that they might not turn up, so I decided on a nursery because, firstly, they'll take my children at short notice for a short time; secondly, they're open from 8 am to 6 pm; and thirdly, they take babies from one month old.'

Janine, 37, doctor

'They go to the school where I teach. I only work during school hours so I have no costs and no worries!'

Ingrid, 35, teacher

'I chose my mother to look after Martin because she was the only person I felt comfortable leaving him with. I knew she would give him security, love and devotion.'

Sarah, 26, florist/student

'One of the best benefits of working full time is that my husband collects the children from school, so on some evenings I can go for a swim or go shopping on my own. I have more time, more control and, best of all, more money!'

Lynda, 41, marketing executive

'I'm not happy with my childcare arrangements. At the moment my sister-in-law has my child three days and my mum one day a week. My sister-in-law's views on childcare are different to mine but it's hard to make her change because she's family.'

Caren, 31, group accountant

'I use the workplace nursery, at £76 per week for a subsidized place. The nursey was set up while I was on maternity leave. I am happy because I am only 20 yards away from Joseph all day, and it completely covers all my shifts. The down side is that I have to commute with him.'

Isobel, 31, psychiatric ward sister

'The nursery is near my work and my mother, and my daughters' schools are at the end of my mother's road. If she hadn't been living nearby, I would never have been able to go back to work after my daughters were born: childcare costs would have completely swallowed up my part-time earnings.'

Joanna, 37, local government officer

'There is a mutual trust between myself and my childminder; we have never let each other down. I'm very fortunate, though, to have someone prepared to childmind between 7 am and 8 pm!'

Elizabeth, 38, care assistant/Project 2000 trainee

'My husband is a self-employed upholsterer working from our home. His work dropped off somewhat during the recession,

so when our daughter was born it seemed a good idea for me to return to work and for him to look after our daughter.'
Alexandra, 37, computer systems analyst

'After-school club for 10 hours (at £25 a week). A friend worked there on the staff and it's near my office. The quality of care and facilities are good.'
Judy, 39, customer service manager

'We have a nanny four days a week and our child goes to grandmother on the fifth day. Our nanny works 38 hours for £110 a week clear. She was recommended to us by friends. She had been their nanny but their son was starting school. I could not have anyone better looking after our baby.'
Audrey, 41, admin supervisor

'I have an au pair. She works between 20 and 25 hours a week for £40 plus keep. Au pairs are the cheapest form of childcare. I use an agency: the German YMCA. The only problem is that every September, when the new au pair arrives, I have to start all over again.'
Christine, 42, resource manager (publications)

'Grandparents. The arrangement is fine, although I sometimes feel that our baby is missing out on contact with other children.'
Julie, 29, accountant

'My mum had been made redundant and, at 50, she didn't want to go back to full-time work. We needed a childminder. So we pay her £50 a week and that solves both problems.'
Sally, 24, library assistant

'I don't think I could have returned to work and left our children with anyone other than my husband. We wanted one of us to have that close emotional bond which comes from daily interaction.'

Joy, 36, teacher

'I have a mother's help, who does 20 hours a week for £250 a month. She answered our advertisement in the local paper and we liked her immediately.'

Wendy, 35, nursing sister

'I never had anyone to look after them. I always raced home before school was out.'

Elizabeth, 51, fine art journal editor

'I consulted the register issued by the local authority. My choice of childminder was guided by the fact that she told me it was the guinea pig's birthday on the day we were planning to meet (it was marked on the calendar).'

Stella, 35, housing manager

'Nursery from 9 am to 6 pm, Monday to Friday. That is forty-five hours. It costs £780 for two each month.'

Monica, 44, range manager

'The children spend two full days in a crèche, costing £16 per child per day. The crèche is only 100 yards away and it's well run. I wanted a structured day for the children which you don't get with a childminder. I am quite happy with the arrangement, but full-time childcare is more expensive than a second mortgage.'

Sheelagh, 33, accountant

What sort of good/bad childcare experiences have you had?

'I don't really trust childminder registers any more; I prefer word of mouth. I had a bad experience with someone I chose from a register once. I used to arrive to collect my daughter (then aged 18 months) and she would run out crying and cling to me. And she hated being left in the mornings. Things finally came to a head at the childminder's son's birthday party. Siobhan was left to play in a paddling pool all afternoon wearing only knickers. The sun block I had supplied hadn't been used – "because there's a lot of cloud", I was told, and her bunches hadn't even been taken out; she had two-inch blisters all round the top of her ears and was severely sunburnt everywhere else.'

Beverley, 28, civil servant

'My husband looks after our children or, if we're both working, a NNEB qualified nanny comes to our house for approximately 15–20 hours a week. We did not have to advertise because I was introduced to Andrea through her mother. I'm very happy with the way things have worked out. My husband is excellent with the children and Andrea is committed and treats them as if they were her own. That enables me to concentrate at work and not have to worry about their welfare, safety and happiness. We feel Andrea is our Mary Poppins. Don't judge people by appearances, the person inside is much more important.'

Angela, 31, police officer

'I couldn't work without my wonderful mother's support. I only wish I could repay her in more ways than I'm able to. I couldn't be happier with my childcare arrangements.'

Janice, 32, in a credit accumulation/transfer scheme

'With my first child, I rang the childminder unexpectedly. She had gone out leaving my two-year-old with her 10-year-old. It may only have been for a minute but that was the end of a beautiful friendship.'

Lynne, 33, student

'I have been let down by one nanny; she left my 18-month-old alone on a dual carriageway!'

Tina, 37, civil servant

'My childminder is the best in the world. She's a good friend who actually asked if she could look after my baby before I went back to work; her girls had gone to school and she missed them. She is now fully registered, and she does more with my children than I would ever do.'

Linda, 39, saddler

'The first childminder I had didn't communicate very much; she always had my daughter bundled up and waiting by the door when I arrived. I didn't know how long she had been waiting for me to arrive. It was a horrible feeling. In contrast, Lori's childminder is wonderful. It's Lori's second home. If ever I have a problem getting home on time, I never have to worry that the childminder will view it badly.'

Jane, 35, PR/marketing manager

'I had terrible experiences when I was going out to work after the birth of my first child. One nanny even turned out to have a police record for violence and yet I hired her through an agency.'

Sally, 39, composer

'I am very happy with my childcare arrangements. Having a live-in nanny means that you really know your child's carer and vice versa. It gives us great flexibility and it means that we have a built-in babysitter. She is very well qualified and capable.'

Janet, 35, veterinary surgeon

'One childminder let me down while I was checking her references; she made arrangements with another mum who was happy to accept her without references.'

Kathleen, 36, human resources adviser

'I have had nannies steal from me and lie to me; I think nurseries/childminders are much better. Because Sam is developmentally retarded, the special needs nursery school is exactly what he needs, and his childminder gives him a "normal" home environment in which to relax in the afternoon.'

Jenny, 27, systems analyst/IT manager

'I am very happy with the nursery I've found because Evie is well looked after, her food is nutritionally balanced and she gets education through play. She has interaction with other children there and the education is wonderful. Obviously, although these benefits are for her, her being happy makes me happy too.'

Sarah, 25, general manager of retail/mail-order leisurewear company

'I had an upsetting experience with one childminder. I interviewed her twice at her home and spoke to her on the telephone. I was about to pay my deposit when I talked to the mum of another child looked after by the childminder and discovered that she had an Alsatian dog which had never been mentioned, and had obviously been hidden on my visits. This really upset me because I felt that I had been on the point of leaving my daughter with someone who was prepared to deceive me.'

Kathryn, 32, senior computer programmer/analyst

'I'm extremely happy with my childcare arrangements. I can depend on both my childminder and the nursery totally. Having both works very well for us because of the mix of family and home environments – plus the excitement and stimulation of a nursery.'

Mary, 46, customer services manager.

'My children are at school now, but I used to have a nanny. I interviewed 80 people and found only one potentially suitable candidate, and she turned out to be a drunken driver. She wrote off her car and it transpired that she had been three times over the alcohol limit. I was horrified to think that my children might have been in the car!'

Susan, 45, student/company director

'I interviewed one unsuitable woman. The first reason she gave for wanting to childmind was the money and the second was to be at home with her husband; there was no mention of enjoying children!'

Nicola, 29, antique furniture restorer

'I know that my child is being cared for in a happy, supportive environment, and most of all that she's happy. When I took maternity leave this time, she was very keen to keep going to nursery to see her friends, rather than staying at home with me!'

Kate, 30, charity manager

'Normally my parents cared for my six-year-old son. There was one day, however, when my husband had an important exhibition in London that he wanted me to be present at; it was a school day and my parents had no transport. I made arrangements for another working mother, who lived nearby, to collect him with her daughter; he would go back to her house for tea. When I got back home at 9.30 pm, I rushed round to collect him from my friend to find they were out. Puzzled, I telephoned her mother-in-law, because I knew that she assisted with childcare. I was greeted by a stunned silence and then an "Oh no!". Apparently, something had gone wrong at work for my friend and she had asked mum-in-law to collect both children but she'd forgotten. I was frantic by this stage, but I telephoned the headmaster of the school and thankfully he was able to tell me that he had my son with him. When I got to his house, I expected tears and a very sad little boy, but instead there he was, giving a concert for the headmaster and his family on their grand piano. He sauntered over to me, gave me a big hug, and said "What's all the fuss for? I knew you'd come sometime." I couldn't believe his faith in me.'

Charlotte, 50, probation officer

'My mother looks after Simon. My parents live nearby and Simon loves spending time with his grandparents and has bonded so well with them over the years that it's worked out wonderfully for all of us.'

Sue, 35, training manager

'I had a "nanny from hell". She was so "frank" that she upset most of my neighbours, and my one-year-old child gradually grew more and more unhappy in her care. The last straw was when she demanded a pay rise after I had had to take a pay cut in a new job having been made redundant. Neighbours later told me that she had not only shouted at my son, but had slapped him too.'

Mary, 34, business analyst (IT)

'I found young nannies useless, even NNEB ones. They were very precious about what they were and were not prepared to do. I had about eight young girls in quick succession. There were several car crashes, no-shows and other similar horrors; they were totally unreliable. Then I advertised locally (forget the Kensington nanny agency!) and found a woman with an 18-year-old daughter of her own. She was totally different. She just felt like a mum. She never let me down and she got a genuine kick out of kids and has kept in touch since she's left. The younger ones were more interested in Neighbours – my toddlers would groan when they heard the theme tune – and boyfriends than children. I've had two of these wonderful women now, for about three years each – perfect.'

Lesley 41, publisher

'I have come across an unsuitable nursery in the past: staff shouting at each other and uninterested children. We left after six weeks and William went to an excellent nursery further from home until we moved.'

Julia, 35, patent analyst

'I was very lucky with childminders. The first one was okay but she didn't want to carry on when I went back into the office after five months. The next was really good and, as David was the only child she looked after, she took him everywhere and he was more like part of the family. She had pets too, which was nice for David because we don't have any. She still looks after David during the school holidays.'

Jayne, 35, manager

'I have been badly let down by two childminders. The first was my sister-in-law who left my 18-month-old son alone for a whole morning. He took tablets from her bag and swallowed them all, which has left him with a damaged kidney. I then obtained a local authority register and vetted several registered childminders until I felt that I had chosen the right person. She had four children of her own, all at secondary school, but she left my son in the sun all day to get sunstroke. She didn't change his nappy or keep him clean and sometimes he came home with cuts and bruises, which could have been prevented.'

Sue, 36, general manager/part-time student

'I have been badly let down by two au pairs: one was out when my youngest child came home from school; the other proved to be mentally unsuitable.'

Miranda, 39, manager of workplace nursery

How do you cover the holidays?

'During school holidays, my daughter has a variety of carers which can be difficult to organize, but I am fortunate to have teenage sisters who help. My daughter likes all her carers. A full-time nanny would be better but I cannot afford one!'

Jane, 25, housing officer

'I have quite a lot of problems during school holidays, because there are no after-school playschemes in my area. My husband and I stagger our holidays and my mother helps.'

Kendra, 32, secretary

'My children attend the school where I teach, so the great advantage is that I'm at home during the holidays. I have no costs and no worries.'

Ingrid, 35, school teacher

'There is nothing worse than knowing that all your children's friends are going off to the beach, or somewhere nice during the holidays, while your own children either have to come in to work with you or to go to a minder.'

Jayne, 38, estate agent

'The high cost of holiday activity schemes makes things difficult. These things cost about £100 a week.'

Judy, 39, customer service officer

'My husband takes time off but that means that we don't often get holidays all together as a family.'

Janice, 37, midwife

'During school holidays I have to look after the children and work from home – usually in the evenings or at weekends.'

Helen, 38, solicitor

'The problem during school holidays is trying to keep them occupied, rather than drifting onto the streets for want of anything better to do.'

Janice, 43, accountant

'My nine-year-old has outgrown her childminder. She gets bored during the school holidays. The benefits for me, though, are that she is safe and I have peace of mind.'

Patricia, 39, operating theatre sister (RGN)

'I don't have any problems during the school holidays. There are various playschemes, football and sports courses – and they have friends who also have working mothers – so they swap bases.'

Gillian, 48, accounts manager

'I use a student during the holidays; she works for fourteen hours at £1.50 an hour, and she is great. She was recommended by another parent. She comes to the house and is nearer the children's ages.'

Angela, 38, part-time clerical officer

Is having more than one child easier or more difficult to manage?

'It's much more difficult; it feels like a juggling act. If only the playschemes were for longer hours.'

Di, 30, quality control supervisor

'It's no more difficult having three than one; the only problems occur when all three of them have to be in different places at the same time. But we manage.'

Pam, 32, wedding photographer

'Financially, it's very hard. They're in separate nurseries and we pay £700 a month while I work for a pittance.'

Carol, 33, police officer.

'It has been relatively easier for me because there are seven years between my daughters and Emma has always been a great help.'

Irene, 42, hotelier

'It is much more difficult to manage two, especially if they don't seem to need any sleep. My daughter, now 22 months, still goes down regularly at 10.30 pm, and she never has more than thirty minutes sleep in the day.'

Brenda, 33, business development manager

'Coordinating collection is complicated and tiring. And if I have to work from home with the children, it is difficult to supervise them because they are different ages and want to do totally different things.'

Arabella, 33, interior designer

'More than one means that usually they occupy each other. One child to dress takes only marginally less time than two, and they soon help each other. When cooperation fails, logistics become dodgy.'

Judith, 36, chartered physiotherapist

'Yes, it's difficult to get Hannah to school, Liam to nursery and still be at work on time. And if one child is unwell, it throws everything into chaos.'

Karen, 32, accountant

'Yes. People are more likely to look after one. Two often makes people more reluctant.'

Donna, 30, registered nurse (for the mentally handicapped)

'No, it makes no difference now they are both at school. It was hell when one was at school and the other at nursery: I must have done three times the mileage I do now.'

Lucy, 38, secretary/personal assistant & research interviewer

'Yes, sometimes it seems as though they are never both well at the same time.'

Sue, 36, deputy head teacher

'At times it's more tiring: the morning and teatime rushes are hard work, for instance. My partner works shifts so is rarely there to help. I have to get up at 6.30 am to get out of the house by 8 am.'

Anita, 35, software engineer

Tips – for all carers

1. Look at all the different options; think them through carefully; and do not make hasty decisions.

2. Interview thoroughly with a list of set questions. Follow your instincts and see how the carer interacts with your child; but take up references too.

3. Have a changeover book so that when your child is not with you, you are still aware of what he has been doing/eating.

4. Choose a carer that suits your lifestyle best and pay her/him as well as you can afford to; she/he is looking after your most treasured possession.

5. Ensure that you and your carer have the same views on discipline, diet and potty training etc.

6. Ensure that your child will be able to socialize with other children.

Au pairs

1. Insist that they speak good English or you speak their language.

2. If you use an agency, ask for details of a selection of girls.

3. If you can afford to, offer to pay your au pair's travel costs if she/he stays with you the agreed length of time. In this way you will greatly reduce the chances of them rushing home early.

4. Take time to help them settle down; they can be terribly homesick.

5. Don't use an au pair instead of a proper experienced carer. They are not qualified to look after babies or toddlers

for long periods and it is unfair to expect them to shoulder too much responsibility.

6. Check whether they know how to cook simple meals; find out whether they smoke. Have they lived away from home before? What experience have they had? etc.

Nanny

1. Ask for two written references but do not rely on these alone, because they can conflict with what someone might say on the telephone.

2. Don't assume that an agency knows a nanny as well as they say.

3. Try to get someone who has been recommended, and who thinks as you do.

4. Check to see how long they have been with their present family and why they are leaving. What sort of activities/outings would they arrange? Are they insured? Do they have a clean driving licence? Are they trained in First Aid? Have they a criminal record? Has a child ever come to harm in their care?

5. Watch the nanny with your child for a few days before going back to work.

Childminder

1. Only choose a childminder who is registered with Social Services, and trust your gut feeling about him/her.

2. Your child's behaviour will show you if he is happy there.

3. If the minder has children, are they well-mannered, happy etc.?

4. Don't look for a tidy house (but do not ignore one that is too messy).

5. Ask to see up-to-date insurance paperwork.

6. Check whether she or her partner smokes. Will she be able to fit in with your working hours? How many other children does she care for and what are their ages? What kind of activities/outings will she arrange?

7. Check to see if the childminder's garden is fenced off.

8. Ask whether the childminder has dogs and, if so, whether they are exercised in the park or child's play area in the garden

Nurseries

1. Random checking on nurseries reveals the true story. Look to see if the children are happy. Are there several small activity areas? Is it bright and cheerful? What is the ratio of staff to children? What meals do they serve? What do they do about discipline?

2. One advantage of having your child at a nursery rather than with a childminder is that you cannot leave your child with a minder if she or her children are ill, while nurseries can easily cope with staff illness.

Single

'The love I get from my children makes it all worthwhile.'

Lone parents are singled out for a lot of criticism by the British Government and the press, but most single mothers did not intend to bring up their child alone. They were either married or living with the father of their child when, for whatever reason, the relationship ended.

Anyone who thinks that single parents have an easy life 'sponging off the State', as the tabloids are so fond of saying, should try to imagine how they would manage being solely responsible for all the bills and all the decisions – domestic, work and childcare. Anyone whose partner works away from home from time to time gets a brief taste of just how hard it is bringing up children alone. Friendship, love and support are the only things that are welcome at all times.

Of the women questioned nine per cent were single parents who were doing their best to give their children loving and secure homes. Apart from financial difficulties, most women said that the worst things about being a lone parent were not having someone to share the decision-making with and not having anyone to give them a big hug at the end of a long day.

On the plus side, however, they said that they did not have to pander to a partner's needs and whims and had a very close relationship with their children.

What are the advantages/disadvantages of being a single mother?

'Advantages: no one to have to cook for, work around, compromise with or feel resentment towards. Disadvantages: no sex. The main difficulty as I see it is how it has affected the children. I firmly believe children should have both parents, and so I believe it's hard for them not to.'

Nicola, 34, air-traffic controller

'It's good to have one set of rules to live by, but on the negative side everything is down to me: from lifts to school, organizing hobbies and outings, to helping with problems and homework.'

Jean, 44, doctors' receptionist/typist

'I was a single parent for three years. It's pure luxury for your child because of the amount of devotion and one-to-one attention you can give, although I feel that not all children benefit. There aren't enough hours in the day to cook, clean, work, and look after a child, so something has to give – with me it was usually the housework.'

Emma, 28, law student

'With three kids I can't think of any advantages. The big disdvantage is that although a father pays no maintenance towards his kids, he is still legally entitled to access. So I am forced to live the farce, whereby he collects Sarah (the only child who will see him) once a fortnight.

'I applied to the Child Support Agency (C.S.A.) and we have had the assessment review, and my ex-husband is now going to a tribunal to get his payments cut, the payments, that is, that he has never made. My only real difficulties are all financial. Because I started work we now get Family Credit. Before I was on Income Support. After Andrew's nursery and petrol expenses, the children and I had £26 a week to live off. Obviously, I couldn't manage.'

Melissa, 36, student teacher/part-time shop assistant

'Childcare is difficult, and there is only one of you to change the sheets when two of them vomit in the middle of the night.'

Deborah, 36, freelance writer/journalist

'My husband is a chief engineer on oil tankers so I'm alone for six months of the year. The big disadvantage is having no one to talk to about small everyday problems, nor anyone to share any nice experiences with the children.'

Ann, 41, chartered accountant

'The advantage is being able to do what you want, when you want with no one to doubt you. You are in complete control. Being single makes you stronger and more determined to get the most out of life. For me, there are no disadvantages.'

Sarah, 26, florist/student

'I am divorced and now have a new partner but we are not as yet living together. When you have a partner, you kid yourself that they are half responsible. Now I know I have to do everything and I make all the decisions. One of my problems is the whole issue of the male role model, because my ex-husband is gay.'

Jenny, 27, systems analyst/IT Manager

'Disadvantages: not having a father figure to take him to football matches ocasionally, etc. I do not have regular partners sleeping at the house; that would confuse him.'

Sue, 35, training manager

'My main advantage is that I don't have to live with an abusive husband any more. The disadvantage is that everything is down to me. My child either has to come everywhere with me or I need a babysitter; even going to the corner shop is a major excursion. And I can't commit myself to any sort of regular social life.'

Di, 30, quality control supervisor

'Disadvantage: you have no one who loves your child as much as you do, with whom to prattle on about the funny things he did last night; the cute comments he made; the big hugs he gives you. Equally, there is no one significant to moan to about his bad points and share your concerns with: Jason is disruptive at school and lacks concentration; he misses his father, although he sees him once a fortnight.

'My life as a single working mother is made easier by: (a) a very supportive boss, (b) a reasonable salary and standard of living, (c) having my office five minutes drive from school which means that I can easily pop over for chats with the teacher, school events etc., (d) the fact that Jason attends a well-run, reliable after-school club, and (e) having like-minded friends who form a mutual support group. When you are a single working mother, you need someone to tell you that you are doing a great job.'

Judy, 39, customer service officer

'I can't think of any advantages of being a single mother. I feel you need the support of a partner to bring up a child successfully.'

Susan, 27, insurance clerk

'Advantage: you feel 21 again; Disadvantage: you know you aren't! Advantage: what you earn is yours; Disadvantage: and your kids. Advantage: you become male/female; Disadvantage: you forget to be fun along the way!'

Jenny, 50, caretaker/domestic engineer

'I'm just getting to grips with being a single parent, although my husband used to work away from home anyway. It's hard having to do it all with the children when you've had a long hard day at work. The main difficulties are tiredness and shortage of cash. I really resent having to pay for babysitters in order to attend evening meetings.'

Allyson, 33, teacher/head of department

'I hate the prejudice you get from married couples.'

Margaret, 23, part-time bank official/fitness instructor

'It can be very draining, especially if you are working and are woken regularly during the night.'

Judy, 37, lecturer/musician

'My partner and I split up two and a half years ago, having been together for 10 years. The combination of my job and my children can be very demanding but it does get easier – and the love you get from your children makes it worthwhile.'

Lorraine, 32, intelligence analyst

'The advantage is that I have a daughter who loves me very much, as I do her. The disadvantages are numerous: total responsibility both financially and emotionally. Who cares for her when I'm sick? When she is ill, I need to arrange to have time off work. It's an emotional roller coaster. I have no family in this country so it really is difficult to juggle everything on my own.'

Jane, 35, public relations/marketing manager

'I feel trapped in a low-paid job but it offers the hours that I need.'

Julie, 35, hand embroiderer

'One disadvantage is not having someone to carry things and lift the baby. I always have aching shoulders.'
Kerry, 36, application support & training
for developing countries

'I like the fact that it doesn't matter now if the cleaning isn't done, or a meal isn't ready on time. Children wait; men don't.'
Heather, 43, teacher

'I have no money and no social life that doesn't involve children. It is amazing how few working single mums there are.'
Beverley, 28, civil servant

'I cannot always afford to buy exactly what I want for my children.'
Angela,31, fundraiser

'Advantage: no man to worry about, so you only have to divide yourself into two instead of three. Disadvantage: lack of moral and financial support. Right now I'm in a second unhappy marriage, with a man whom my son dislikes, but with a new baby too. Do I make do, or try and go it alone again?'
Jayne, 38, estate agent

Tips

1. Organize your day/week/month ahead of time. Try to consolidate jobs where possible and get into a good working routine which suits both you and your child.

2. Establish a mutual support system with friends/ relations who are also single mothers. See if you can swap baby-sitting/ staying overnight with them.

3. Don't spoil children as they easily become demanding.

4. Let some chores go – don't try to do it all.

5. Don't forget your own interests. As a single parent the parent-child relationship is more intense.

6. If you are going through a divorce or are recently bereaved, get advice on benefits, pensions or maintenance payments.

Partner

'He wouldn't have time for an affair.'

'*Mummy, what are you doing?*' Natalie asked, head peering round the bathroom door and nose wrinkled in disgust at the scene that met her eyes.

'*Can't you see I'm cleaning,*' I snapped irritably, as I stood halfway up a stepladder polishing the tiles. At the bottom of the ladder lay dozens of half-full bottles of shampoo, conditioner, bubble bath, baby creams and lotions. The bath and washbasin were covered in foam, waiting to be rinsed off and the air was choking with the acrid fumes of bleach as germs were being vanquished left, right and down the S-bend.

'*But Mummy, you don't like cleaning much, do you?*' she half-whispered, sensing my frustration at being interrupted.

'No, not much.'

'*Well, put that duster down then and let's go play in my tent,*' she continued matter of factly. '*We can get Daddy to do the cleaning later.*'

Do you encourage both your sons and daughters to cook, iron and help with household chores? If not, then how can you expect them to grow up believing that men and women have equal responsibilities around the home?

Of the women surveyed, six per cent complained bitterly about lazy partners who expected them to do a full day's work and then come home, put the children to bed, keep the house clean and have a hot meal ready. Many of these men had had mothers who did everything for them and therefore expected the same treatment from their wives and girlfriends. Luckily, in the 1990s, these men are in the minority as more than half the surveyed women said that their partners helped with the children and all the chores – nine per cent even said that their men did more housework than they did.

Men's attitudes to women working have changed dramatically in the last 20 years as redundancies have slimmed down predominantly male workplaces and more women's jobs have been created – although the majority are part time and not well paid.

More than half of the women have partners who are proud of them and supportive of their chosen career; one fifth said that their job is regarded as a good source of extra income, while 17 per cent feel that their partners don't regard what they do as a proper job.

Of these women's partners, six per cent thought that they weren't being paid enough attention and so turned to other women; 62 per cent of the surveyed women were adamant that their partner would not use their working as an excuse for an affair.

In what ways does your partner contribute towards childcare/the running of your household?

'My husband is an incredibly tidy person, so he doesn't mind sorting out the children's rooms occasionally. I cook for the children, but he likes to cook wonderful meals for us once the children are in bed! As an estate agent, I have to work late sometimes. When that happens, my husband will collect the younger boys, feed all four and put the younger ones to bed.'

Jackie, 36, accounts clerk/estate agent

'My husband was quite unsupportive when we first got married and had our first child. I think he still thought he was single, although he has never been one to go to the pub on his own. I would never have married him if he had been. We had many discussions and arguments and now he makes meals, looks after the girls, and does some housework – if left a list.'

Susan, 37, WP operator/clerk

'He is great. He makes our breakfasts (his, mine, the kids' and the dog's); he makes the bed every morning, does more than half the shopping, makes our packed lunches, clears up after our evening meal, and does some ironing and gardening; and he walks the dog. More than me! He is proud of me working because he thinks it is better for me; we need the money; and it takes the pressure off him.'

Audrey, 41, admin supervisor

'He helps with the housework – but does need prompting. He does DIY and car maintenance. He helps cook. He cares for the children during holidays and weekends, but rarely organizes babysitters or a schedule for holidays. I try to run a household diary for meals and school runs – although he refers to it.'

Judith, 36, chartered physiotherapist

'I'm 48 and my husband is much older than me and severely disabled: he is wheelchair-bound and cannot speak. Obviously, he cannot contribute to the running of the household nor to childcare; he must be dressed and lifted out of bed, lifted on and off the toilet, and into the shower etc. He is a brilliant engineer and runs the research and development end of the business, which grew out of his own disability, but he is physically unable to do anything around the house. Sometimes, I feel like a single parent, albeit one with a very good support system! We live with his elderly parents.'

Sheila, 33, director/company secretary/manufacturer of communication equipt. for people who cannot speak

'He helps up to a point, as long as it doesn't affect anything he wants to do.'

Frances, 38, personal assistant

'He collects the children in the evening, looks after them if I'm on call and helps with the ironing and washing a lot of the time. He is proud of me and my achievements and is usually pretty supportive. He is happy to have the children when I work but he still finds hospital work a little difficult to understand – even after 17 years!'

Janine, 37, doctor

'My son does the cleaning. We all do our own ironing. They do their own rooms. We do a week's menu and one or other child usually helps.'

Jean, 44, senior probation officer

'He's at home for three weekdays and looks after the children, does the housework, prepares meals and washes up. He is proud of my achievements and more ambitious for me than I am for myself.'

Carole, 36, bank manager

'My husband still wants me to do his washing, ironing, wait on him hand, foot and finger, and I get very angry with him. His mother did it because she didn't work, so he expects me to as well. I seem to be an unpaid slave at home – the cost of having a career. We run our company together but if I get the contracts, he plays it down. He wouldn't have any business without me, though.'

Jill, 34, university technician/owner of security business

'He looks after the children while I am at work and cooks some meals. He does more tidying up than I do, although I do more dish- and clothes-washing. I tend to write lists and notice if we are running low on something, although now, after nearly two years as a "house husband", he is beginning to think ahead a bit more. He has taken five years off work to look after the children so that I can pursue my career.'

Rebecca, 30, district forester

'He works part time to have more time for the family. He does almost all the childcare, most of the cooking, all the cleaning and half the washing and ironing. I shop alone while he takes the children swimming.'

Isobel, 40, senior civil servant

'When Rachel was born, Dave was a tremendous support and did everything. But as I got back to normal he started to do less and less, and while I was at home all the time I didn't mind. Once I went back to work, though, I was still doing everything, so after a while I kept a list of all the things we each did around the house – even to the smallest things like remembering the milk order and locking up at night. The huge imbalance surprised even me and I showed it to Dave to make a point. I think it worked.'

Kaye, 31, senior accounts manager

Do you shop together, alone or with the children?

'We go together. I'm responsible for preparing the list.'

Catherine, 39, senior secretary

'We hardly ever shop together. One of us does it without the children.'

Judy, 36, guidance officer/secretary

'William shops. I refuse because I do everything else. He wants food, he shops. Unless I am entertaining, that is: then I shop and I pay.'

Linda, 39, saddler

'I take responsibility for household shopping because I can order all the food from my suppliers.'

Karen, 28, caterer

'My husband does the shopping with the children. I am the major breadwinner at present. He was while I was building up my career. He is very proud of me, but occasionally feels inadequate.'

Sally, 39, composer

'My husband will do a big shop once or twice a month at Sainsbury's because he has the car. I do fill-in shopping at local shops. I don't shop by mail order but if I could ring Sainsbury's, tell them what I want, and they would deliver, it would be great.'

Jayne, 35, manager

'I shop with my son because he loves sitting in a trolley and eating fresh French bread as we go around. My partner is very *supportive and has helped me a lot in becoming self-employed; looking after the tax details, researching the best office equipment, even decorating the study.'*

Claire, 34, marketing consultant

'I do the household shopping. He is a social phobic and can suffer from agoraphobia in crowds.'

Mary, 34, business analyst

How does your partner regard your career?

'He regards it as secondary to his, but is glad of the additional income. It is tolerated only while it does not clash with his schedule.'

Lesley, 40, photographer/book-keeper

'He expects me to work, as he is self-employed. I was the main earner during the recession and still am now. Sometimes I feel he is not as motivated to work because he knows I will always be earning. I have tried nagging, to no avail, and have had to take time off work because of stress/anxiety/depression caused by trying to do too much.'

Lynda, 34, registered nurse

'My partner would rather I was at home, but knows we couldn't manage. He is quite jealous of my success because he is unemployed most of the time. Sometimes I feel I would be better off financially on my own, but we have a good relationship and children etc. I wish he could be successful because I would be happier then too.'

Linda, 39, saddler

'He's very grateful to me for working at the nursing home, as it helps financially, and is extremely proud of me for going to university. He's hoping I'll get a decent job at the end of it all so that we can have a better life. But if I don't, he'd still be proud of me.'

Helen, 32, staff nurse/full-time student

'He is wholly supportive, but would definitely prefer me to be at home: show me a man who wouldn't!'

Catherine, 28, branch administrator

'He married me as an intelligent career woman – children are the icing on the cake. He is very supportive and would be unhappy if I gave up work to look after the children full time.'

Mary, 56, customer services manager

'He says he is supportive and proud, but when my daughter said she wanted to become a beauty therapist and work with me, he told her she was clever enough to get a proper job.'

Wendy, 36, beauty therapist

'My husband works very hard doing long hours in order for me to continue my degree, and jokes that he will retire when I've qualified. But I know he would not be happy if he wasn't working at all. He does not earn a brilliant salary, and I will more than likely earn more than him, but he is extremely supportive and says he is proud of me.'

Lynne, 33, student

'Initially, he wanted me to give up work, as we had planned, after baby number two. But after he saw how depressed I was at home (with anti-depressants prescribed), he wanted me to get back to my "old self" as soon as possible, and supported me all the way.'

Diane, 29, insurance underwriter

'We are a unit; we both contribute. He is very supportive and thinks that my career is as important as his own. He has refused overtime because of my emergency duties; he told his boss exactly why and he is respected for it.'

Margaret, 47, senior medical laboratory scientific officer

'We're equal partners and earn the same. He couldn't support our standard of living without my salary, and respects me for the responsible job I do.'

Wendy, 35, nursing sister

'He hated the fact that I became independent from him – mentally and financially – and was very jealous because I earned more than him.'

Joanna, 43, casualty nurse

'Because my husband is at university, he is able to be involved in childcare and household duties. He now sees me as the main breadwinner, which is a bit scary.'

Claire, 36, social worker

'He feels that my career is vital for me. He's proud of my work and knows it is very satisfying to me.'

Lynn, 41, occupational therapist

'When he didn't work, he expected me to bring in the money while he put his feet up.'

Fiona, 40, health visitor

'He regards my career as a vital source of income. He is very proud of my achievements and successes, and believes that we should share the children 50:50. Unfortunately, the chores split more 80:20, with the bulk falling my way.'

Rona, 28, researcher for executive search agency

'He was very proud when I passed my first-year exams in Personnel Management, but sees my job as secondary to his, because he earns more.'

Joanne, 26, personal assistant

'He sees the income as essential (so do I), but when I first went back to office work, he was irritable and very unsupportive. Although he encouraged me to study for exams, it seemed as though I still had to perform all the other tasks to keep the house running as well. His attitude became more flexible once I had accepted a full-time job.'

Lynda, 41, marketing executive

'He is proud of me but because he doesn't see what I do and because I don't earn much, as I am still building up pupil numbers, I think he sometimes forgets that I work – and I'm studying for a degree too – and he can't understand if the house is a mess.'

Alison, 37, self-employed music teacher

'I never particularly wanted a career and over the past two years things have just developed. My husband cannot believe that this woman, who wasn't particularly keen to work, is now more enthusiastic about it than he is – and earns more!'

Paula, 31, GP and police surgeon

'He would never admit it but he's happy for me to earn the main income. But he likes to look as though he is.'

Jayne, 38, estate agent

'He doesn't really think of it as my career, but values it for the additional income. Probably it isn't as important as his job. It is something else to do but shouldn't interfere with looking after him.'

Mary, 51, government press officer

Do you ever worry about your partner using your working as an excuse to have an affair?

'My husband only thinks about work. He wouldn't have time for an affair.'

Joy, 41, general assistant/business proprietor/care assistant

'With hindsight, I think he did. I trained as a nurse to enable me to be financially independent, ready for the day when I could divorce him and support myself and the kids.'

Joanna, casualty nurse

'If you met Thomas, you'd know why I'm smiling. Thomas and I view adultery as the final insult. The way in which he loves me I have no worries. My ex-husband, however, shagged for England!'

Emma, 28, undergraduate law student

'I don't have to worry about him having an affair; I can keep an eye on him because we work together!'

Jackie, 36, accounts clerk/estate agent

'No, but I damaged our relationship while I fought hard to re-establish my independence and place in the world.'

Lynda, 41, marketing executive

'No, I did not worry and I do not now. I was the one who went astray. My second husband was very introverted and unsupportive and I had an eight-year affair with a judge before meeting the man who has now become my third husband.'

Charlotte, 50, probation officer

'My husband is good-looking with a nice personality and I do worry about him meeting someone else, but he has never given me any cause for concern.'

Karen, 28, caterer

'No, although I sometimes worry because I have less time for him. Indeed, I sometimes feel his needs come last – after the baby and the dog.'

Audrey, 41, admin supervisor

'I used to wonder if he was having an affair because he's at home and in a woman's world now, meeting so many women at the school etc. The opportunity is definitely there while I'm working. But now, after a few rows, I trust him. He knows other women are all out of bounds.'

Joy, 36, teacher

'No. He is a solicitor too and we have both seen the distress caused to families (through our work) when one partner goes "astray". We couldn't do it to our children.'

Joanna, 37, local government officer (former solicitor)

'No, he hasn't got time to have an affair. He also knows that I wouldn't tolerate it, and he's a man with a healthy respect for the safety of his private parts!'

Jill, 39, university administrator

'No, I don't worry. I don't own him. When I am working he is minding the children. If he still has the energy, then full marks!'

Patricia, 39, operating theatre sister (RGN)

'Yes, I do, because it has happened. He still works in the same place as her.'

Carrie, 43, deputy head teacher

'I sometimes worry that I am too tired to give him all the attention I'd like to. But I have no doubts about his loyalty – just his overall happiness.'

Coralie, 23, personal assistant

'It happened in some ways: my ex- used to accuse me of liking my job more than him.'

Heather, 31, specialist nurse

'No, this is the one area he's never given me any worries, although he does "bog off" to the pub too much when I'm working in the evening. I hate that.'

Allyson, 33, teacher/head of department

'No, I trust him. He would not need to use my work as an excuse because he is often abroad on business, for up to two weeks at a time. I just hope it wouldn't come to that.'

Claire, 34, marketing consultant

'No, he adores me! He also values my earning potential and loves my son.'

Kim, 36, lecturer/practitioner (NHS) & advocate for elderly persons

'I don't think we can ever be complacent about relationships. Last year a crisis in our relationship precipitated a long and very open discussion about how my work affects our marriage.'

Elizabeth, 51, fine art journal editor

'No, I had some minor doubts when he started university two years ago, because of all the younger available females, but don't worry about it at all now.'

Jill, 36, general manager/part-time student

'No, because I think me having my job means we keep our relationship fresh.'

Janet, 35, veterinary surgeon

'My husband did!'

Nicola, 34, air-traffic controller

'No, because he's as knackered as I am! He is also a very loyal and honourable man and values his family responsibilities. I think this may be partly because he is a slightly older father; our first child was born when he was 37, the second when he was 40.'

Kate, 30, charity manager

'Yes, I do, because he has a mistress and has been having an affair for the past three years. He's unemployed and my job is seen as necessary for keeping the household together. He's jealous because I seem to find it easier to get a job than he does. He did not like the extra activities, like Brownies or fundraising that needed my time.

'He now only sees his mistress on Sundays, when they go walking. I know he would like more: weekends away, for instance, but I've begun to get strict and have told him that if he goes away on a weekend with her, he can stay away. He thinks that's unfair and it makes him feel trapped, but I think he's bloody lucky that I haven't chucked him out, given the way he's behaved. I've lost three and a half stone and still get very upset when I think about them together, but our marriage is stronger now than it was before. We talk more, spend more time together and get on better. Sex is certainly better. I suppose he is using me as a stable home – having his cake and eating it – but I love him and pity him in a way. He's going through a major life crisis: male menopause.'

Jan, 43, hotel manager

Tips – for dealing with an unsupportive partner

1. Communication is essential. Discuss problems and tell him how you feel.

2. If you need more help, ask him. Men don't always notice what needs to be done unless they're told.

3. Start as you mean to go on. Don't treat him as another child; he is not your responsibility.

4. Make a list of all the things you feel you do and get him to do the same.

5. If appropriate, point out all the things that you couldn't have without your income: holidays, meals out, childcare etc.

6. Be clear about how you feel and explain it calmly and assertively.

7. Be clever and invent ways to get round him, if straightforward demands and complaints usually result in him refusing to cooperate. Introduce a barter system.

8. Don't make a habit of sacrificing your happiness to appease your partner; realize that you have your own life to lead too. Get him to try to understand and accept your needs.

9. Get support from elsewhere, including professional counselling, if you need it.

10. Go away for a short period. It can help him appreciate all the unseen work and planning that you do.

11. If all else fails, leave him.

Sex

'We try to get it over with quickly, so that I can sleep.'

'I haven't got a willy, have I, Mummy?' Natalie pronounced, after studying her skinny body in front of the mirror from all angles, pulling and prodding at the more interesting bits.

'No, darling, you haven't,' I sighed, inwardly cursing, but trying to smile sweetly as if it was the first, rather than the tenth time, that we'd covered this anatomical ground that week. 'Little girls and women don't have willies.'

'No, you haven't got a willy, Mummy; Rebecca hasn't got a willy; Loran hasn't . . .'

'That's right,' I interrupted, patience waning by the second.

'Daddy's got a willy though, hasn't he? Leeroy's got a willy as well and Robert and Tony and . . .'

'Yes, all men and boys have. Now how about getting dressed and having some breakfast?' I suggested, hoping to have laid the "who has and hasn't got a willy" debate to rest for yet another day by switching to her favourite subject: food.

'Yes, Mummy. Let's go and have breakfast NOW,' she said, excitedly racing for the stairs. She'd only gone down two stairs when a sudden thought stopped her in her tracks. *'Daddy's willy looks like a sausage, doesn't it?'*

'Sex, what's that? I go to bed to sleep,' confessed just under half the women to whom I spoke, who said that they were too tired for sex most of the time.

Many said that they wanted to keep the flames of intimacy and sexual desire flickering but just did not have the energy. They asked for some tips; perhaps the 17 per cent who said that having a busy, working day stimulated their sex life will be able to provide them.

New parents always joke about how getting up for dawn feeds and pacifying screaming babes play havoc with their libido, but most are able to restart their sex lives six to eight weeks after the baby is born (depending on stitches etc.), although some say it takes a year or more to get back to normal.

Nearly a quarter of those polled said that having children had badly affected their sex lives; 39 per cent said that sex had become less frequent, but they knew that this would only be temporary and didn't mind. Some seven per cent, however, said that they were now having better sex than they'd ever had before!

While sex may not be at the top of every couple's 'to do' list, spending time together is recognized as vital to a relationship, and 37 per cent of the women revealed that they regularly and actively set aside time to chat to and cuddle their partners. Just under a quarter said that they only managed to do this sometimes, when other pressures allowed.

Time spent alone together over a meal and a bottle of wine is definitely preferred to the 'expense and hassle' of arranging babysitters for nights out. More than a quarter of the women said that they hardly ever went out alone with their partner; 15 per cent admitted that they only managed to do so on birthdays and anniversaries; while 14 and 22 per cent made the effort once a week and once a month respectively.

Do you and your partner make time to be together?

'Yes, we arrange for our son to visit his grandparents for a few days once every three to four months so that we can have a weekend alone. We go out for the night together twice a month on average. In the short term, we have to make more of the opportunities available.'

Claire, 34, marketing consultant

'We got to a point where we were passing each other through the door; as one went in, the other went out. Then we decided that enough was enough, and have made more time for each other. We hardly ever go out as just the two of us, though.'

Francesca, 31, horse breeder/business partner

'We try to make time to be together. I come home after work sometimes when I know he is home and we make love in the afternoon. We go out when we can: once a month on average for the evening, and once a year for a romantic weekend away. Most of the time we can't have sex on the spur of the moment. It gets quite calculated. We do it more often at bedtime – when I'm tired – and try to get it over with quickly, so that I can sleep!'

Susan, 37, WP operator/clerk

'We never go out – what would we talk about? Children have abolished our sex life.'

Angela, 37, services manager

'We go out at least one night a week, but we never go away at weekends as we feel we need to spend time with Charlotte because she is at nursery all week.'

Karen, 28, caterer

'When I was married, I tried, but he wasn't interested. I later found out why: he is gay! Now my new partner and I both see spending time together as essential. I only had one weekend alone with my ex-husband in two and a half years. Now my mother will have Sam, so we get time for ourselves about once every couple of months.'

Jenny, 27, systems analyst/IT manager

'We try to be on our own together at least two or three evenings a week. The first/second year of each child affected our sex life – I was too tired! – but after that it gradually improved.'

Judy, 36, guidance officer/secretary

'Rarely. I realized just how unsupportive/selfish he was and went off him totally.'

Di, 30, quality control supervisor

'My boyfriend and I go out together regularly and he comes round nearly every day. We go out together, at least every other weekend, because my daughter goes to stay with her father. We try to go away once or twice a year.'

Jane, 25, housing officer.

'Yes, we do make time to be together. We don't watch much television, so our evenings are spent talking etc.'

Jane, 29, office administration manager

'My parents used to babysit (his are both dead and he's an only child) when we went out, but we decided that they were interfering, so now we don't go out. I need to get out and he doesn't, so we have massive problems. To be quite honest, I've had enough and would like to be on my own – with the kids, of course.'

Susan, 42, biomedical scientist (microbiology)

'Yes, although I often have to work late, we don't let it ruin our sex life. I bought him a year's subscription to the Adult Satellite Channel for Father's Day, to keep him awake until I go to bed. We have one weekend away in the winter every year, with our best friends and no children.'

Pam, 32, wedding photographer

'We go out alone every week for a meal and go walking at the weekend whenever we can. We go away for a weekend at least once a month between April and October. We have to sneak out like teenagers now that our children are grown up. Sunday afternoons when they are all out is a godsend!'

Toni, 39, NHS senior manager

'Yes, we go out fairly regularly without the children. We send them upstairs, if not to bed, to their (well-equipped) rooms by 9.30 pm.'

Margaret, 47, senior medical laboratory scientific offficer

'We feel it is very important to make time to be together. We plan holidays and weekends without the children – hence the need for a nanny. Our sex life has had to take a back seat for the moment. Work and children don't allow us much energy for anything else.'

Jackie, 36, accounts clerk/estate agent

How has having children affected your sex life – in the short term and in the long term?

'We only have one bedroom, so we have to be quieter or use the living room. Breast-feeding changed things for me; I find it harder to get in the mood, but my feelings are more intense once I am. The mind/spirit is willing, but the flesh is knackered. We talk about what we will do next time and often it leads to unexpected sex. We play games and dress for each other.'

Tracey, 27, nanny/nursery nurse

'I always enjoyed sex; my husband never seemed to be bothered – probably because he was going astray!'

Jill, 40, sales coordinator

'At first, after Dylan was born, we were both very passionate and I felt especially sensitive whilst I was breast-feeding. I remember my first day home from the hospital: I couldn't wait for Dylan to go to sleep and for us to be left alone. When I stopped breast-feeding, my desires did decrease but only temporarily.'

Carrie, 27, teacher/student.

'It is not as rigorous as it was before the children. I usually go to bed at around 10.30 pm and fall asleep straight away, and our three-year-old climbs into bed with us in the morning, so time to ourselves is more difficult.'

Mary, 56, customer services manager

'I always make the effort and the results are worth it!'

Angela, 31, fundraiser

'A post-natal orgasm has yet to be experienced.'

Penny, 39, freelance journalist/editor

'Short term: my sex drive has increased, I feel more aware of my needs. Long term: having children around can damage your communication and reduce the intimacy between you. You become strangers and it can be very hard to pick up the threads.'

Lynda, 41, marketing executive

'Having children does affect your sex life when they get older too. My daughter was nine years old and had just had a sex lesson at school. My husband went upstairs for something and I took some ironing up, and when we both came down together she said: "Have you just been to have sex?"'

Joy, 41, general assistant/business proprietor/care assistant

'Our sex life is still alive and kicking although we call our daughter "Mobile", standing for mobile contraceptive, as she has a timing knack for wanting a cuddle.'

Wendy, 29, civil servant

'I lost my libido completely after the birth and it has never returned, and our daughter is two and a half years old now. I go through the motions, but would rather sleep!'

Clare, 42, PA/secretary

'Well, I do get told I was more active in my pre-children days, but it's not a bone of contention.'

Julie, 30, business manager.

'Yes, it has a negative effect, but this was never our strongest point. It is not helped by the fact that I still have our child in the bedroom with us. She is good at night but my husband says she puts him off.'

Audrey, 41, admin supervisor

'Our sex life has always been great. We had sex right up to the birth of all three children and, being lucky and never having stitches, have gone back to having sex within two weeks of each birth. We're never too tired for sex. If one of us is very tired, the other one does all the hard work.'

Pam, 32, wedding photographer

'I'm often too tired for sex, but summertime and holidays tend to prompt a revival. Mutual trust and continued love are more important than an active sex life. Quality is more important than quantity!'

Lesley, 40, photographer/book-keeper

'As interested as ever – theoretically at the moment, as there's no partner.'

Judy, 39, customer service officer

'After having my first child, I thought I'd never want sex again! Nowadays we are definitely not a four-to-five-times-a-week couple – more like once a week – but it is enjoyable and satisfying.'

Lynne, 33, student

'Thomas only comes home at weekends, so we used to have an early night on Fridays: no sex, just kissing and cuddling. Then Saturday nights would be late night in the bath, then all night in the bed, candles, massage etc. Children haven't affected our sex life. We grab our chances when we can; we don't just rely on the night, because children being children, they can need us then. If we have a free afternoon, we go for it.'

Emma, 28, undergraduate law student

'In the short term, having children has created a business partnership with my husband and I. We tend to see each other as childminding agents. Because we haven't got much money, we don't use babysitters and therefore we spend our leisure time apart. I believe that this has some effect on our sexual attraction to each other and, ultimately, on our sexual relationship.'

Claire, 36, social worker

'We have less sex now, but the problem is in how we deal with that. For me, it's plenty; for him it's not enough! Twice a week and he's happy; once a week, he's quiet; and once a fortnight, he's moody. I have a problem because my partner is so brilliant that I feel obliged to have sex when I don't want to, or else I feel (rightly or wrongly) that he feels he deserves it after helping me so much, which of course makes me furious and even less in the mood.'

Helen, 32, staff nurse/full-time student

'During pregnancy, it tends to be increased right up to delivery. Whilst breast-feeding, it becomes opportunist, but still regular. Now that we have the bed back to ourselves, we can be imaginative again!'

Judith, 36, chartered physiotherapist

'Yes, Yes, Yes. But a cream bun can taste even better if you don't have it every day! You learn to lick the cream instead of gobbling it up. Love it!'

Angela, 49, antique dealer/bed-and-breakfast business

'I think it's better quality-wise. As far as quantity is concerned, I could never keep up with him before (the stud!)'

Nicola, 36, 2nd year diploma student nurse

'When the children were very young, our sex life was virtually zilch! We were not blessed with angelic babies and they were very demanding. Now our sex life is excellent although, as we work opposing shifts, it is sometimes "by appointment".'

Angela, 31, police officer

'Children remove all spontaneity. There is nothing worse than both of you desperately wanting to make love at 11 o'clock in the morning and knowing that you'll have to wait until 11 o'clock in the evening – by which time both of you are too knackered. We have resorted to stealing a "Do Not Disturb" sign from a hotel, but the kids still try to batter the door down, or the telephone rings. We've even been known to resort to the car locked in the garage!'

Susan, 45, student/company director

'It's virtually non-existent. We have talked about it and both realize that it will improve with time.'

Donna, 30, registered nurse

'A lot less sex, with little innovation or adventurousness. It's usually a quick two-minute missionary position job on a Sunday morning before the kids come barging into the bedroom.'

Cynthia, 40, managing director

'In the short term, children destroyed sex! In the long term, it is now better than ever because when I was pregnant and when the children were babies, we had to find new ways of enjoying ourselves. As the children get older, you get less tired.'

Jill, 39, university administrator

'Having children has totally stopped our sex life. As I've always got on with things, we've grown apart, emotionally and physically. I don't feel close to him, and therefore there is no companionship.'

Sarah, 25, general manager of retail/mail-order leisurewear company

'We've found that our sex life has got better. We can't get down on the kitchen floor during the day, but we can certainly talk about it until the kids go to bed!'

Nadia, 27, student/night care assistant

'I've finally shed four stone which had crept on over some eight years, despite every diet and exercise video going. It turned out to be caused by food intolerances and once I found out which ones they were, the weight fell off gently when I stopped eating the banned foods. I'm back to my old self, which has sparked off an improved sex life and generally higher energy levels. My husband is proud of me, but he never complained or strayed during the awful time when nothing worked to get rid of the weight.'

Terry, 43, photographic goods wholesaler

'Felt pressured for the first two years, but then we were back to normal. And now things are even better, after 22 years of married life.'

Sue, 42, secretary

'As teenagers stay up later and later, there is less opportunity to make good use of the late evenings.'

Tessa, 41, physiotherapist/aromatherapist

'My husband left me for another woman by the time Siobhan was one year old.'

Beverley, 28, civil servant

Are you too tired for sex, or more interested in it because you work and have other interests?

'I'm mainly too tired, although it's improving now the children are older.'

Valerie, 33, part-time special needs assistant

'We're so busy that we're just too tired. But when we do get together, sex is better than it's ever been!'
Catherine, 39, senior secretary

'When I stay at home, I tend not to bother with my appearance. If I dress up and put make-up on to go to work, it gives me more self-confidence, which makes me feel more like sex.'
Sandra, 31, licensee & caterer

'Working with and meeting new people keeps me "alive" and therefore more interested: just because I've bought the goods, it doesn't stop me window-shopping!'
Mary, 51, government press officer

'Often tired. Teachers are often called "term-time virgins", although it's not entirely true.'
Mary, 46, teacher

'Being in the outside world keeps me stimulated and continually updates/refines my self-image. No, I'm not too tired for sex.'
Lynda, 41, marketing executive

'I am tired, but I am aware of the possibility of straying, so I make an effort. I even enjoy it sometimes!'
Linda, 39, saddler

'My partner always seems too tired; I'm the one who needs less sleep. But it's not a big issue to us.'
Sally, 24, library assistant

'There doesn't seem to be any time in which to make time. I'm too tired.'
Joanna, 37, local government officer (former solicitor)

'Being in the "outside" world definitely keeps me more alive and stimulated, but at times I am also very tired. I don't think working makes a huge difference to sex, but it does make you a more interesting person.'

Jackie, 36, accounts clerk/estate agent

'Being in the outside world means you still see yourself as an attractive person.'

Patricia, 39, operating theatre sister (RGN)

'Sometimes I am exhausted, but rarely "too tired" for sex. I feel it is an expression of our closeness, even after a hard day at work. It's the best way to unwind!'

Susan, 27, insurance clerk

'Working part time, I'm less likely to feel like a housework drudge and I'm not so tempted to "let myself go". Facing 40 is tougher.'

Lindsay, 39, supply teacher (former WRAF personnel officer)

'I'm too tired. The outside world makes me feel alive and stimulated – but towards other people. Lots of temptation!'

Julie, 31, careers adviser

'It is easy to say "I'm too tired . . .". You have to make the effort. After a good day at work, we often go to bed when Edward goes to bed and make the most of an early night!'

Jacqueline, 29, personnel officer/PA

Tips for keeping your sex life alive

1. Organize time together (during the day if you cannot go away for a weekend), relaxed and away from children and work.

2. Have the children sleep away for a night or even spend a day with their grandparents.

3. Get your children into an early-bedtime routine.

4. Have an early night yourselves and take a bottle of wine with you.

5. If you are really tired, you can still caress your partner and make him feel good even if you don't want full sex yourself.

6. Try to forget your responsibilities when you are alone together.

7. Don't get into a rut. Experiment a little with different positions and locations.

8. Be opportunist. Don't wait for the perfect setting or moment: enjoy quickies and then relish the times when you have longer together.

9. Use aromatherapy or massage to relax. Bathe together.

10. Make it obvious to your children that you are special to each other and like to be alone at times, even though you love them and enjoy being with them. They will respect your privacy if they also spend time with you.

11. Be honest. Tell your partner what you do and don't enjoy and he will do the same.

12. Remember you are a woman as well as a mother.

13. Put a lock on your bedroom door.

14. Laugh about anything and everything, including sex.

Money

'Children need more than your presence.'

Like it or not, money talks. No, it shouts at most of us. If we are suddenly short of funds, it dictates where we can live, which jobs to accept, which schools our children will attend and, unless an often costly agreement is struck with money's flexible plastic friend, it also stops us flying off for a well-earned break in the sunshine. It also causes more arguments in a relationship than children or work problems. When we've got it, however, almost anything is possible.

Just under one fifth of the women to whom I spoke, though, said that all their money went on childcare and bills, with a further 28 per cent saying that nearly all their money was swallowed up that way. Greater flexibility was achieved by nearly a quarter who pool salaries with their partner.

In the same way that men's attitudes to women working have changed over the last couple of decades, so they are also waking up to women's earning power. A quarter would like/have liked the women in their life to earn more than them and a further 30 per cent said earning less wouldn't bother them at all; only 14 per cent said that they really wouldn't like it.

How does your partner feel about you earning money?

'I think he's sometimes resentful, because I earn the money. So I take control of our finances.'

Tracey, 23, nurse

'My husband feels proud. He says it takes the pressure off him. There's no reason why he should feel any differently about me earning to how I feel about him earning money, and I'm proud of him and glad he has a job – we're a team.'

Audrey, 41, admin supervisor

'His first wife didn't work at all, even when they experienced grave financial difficulties and this put a huge strain on their already troubled marriage.'

Gillian, 35, systems training designer

'We earn the same and he'd love me to get a rise. We earn and spend jointly. Trust is vital. If we both work hard, then he has as many rights to treats as me.'

Julie, 30, business manager

'My partner feels inadequate because I work; he thinks he should be able to afford to "keep" me. He wouldn't like me earning more than him.'

Anne Marie, 31, part-time sales assistant

'He is very encouraging and pleased that I've got some independence, although he sort of expects my money to go into our joint account. It doesn't!'

Valerie, 33, part-time special needs assistant

'When I was married, he detested the idea of me earning money: it meant that I could get out.'

Perianne, 39, interior designer/now a PA

'He knows, and says, that it is an important contribution. But he takes almost complete control of the finances, and emphasizes that we could live off his salary but not mine.'

Carol, 45, teacher

'My husband is very supportive of my ambitions. I give him half my salary and his salary pays all the bills. My son is about to go to boarding school (hairy decision), and I need to work.'

Lindsay, 39, supply teacher (former WRAF personnel officer)

'I don't earn any money because I work in our estate agency. Obviously, if I didn't work, we would have to pay somebody to do my job. The cost of childcare, however, is almost as expensive.'

Jackie, 36, accounts clerk/estate agent

'He feels that I should get adequate renumeration for what I do. Sometimes he feels that I'm not commercially motivated.'

Tessa, 41, physiotherapist/aromatherapist

'He is pleased that I am working, although a lot is spent on childcare and clothes for work! We have a joint account and my salary is "elastic".'

Judy, 37, lecturer/musician

Does he, or would he like it, if you earn/earned more than him?

'I earn more and he feels proud and inadequate at different times.'
Donna, 30, registered nurse (for the mentally handicapped)

'No, he wouldn't like it. All my money goes on bills and childcare: money doesn't buy happiness but it does pay the bloody bills! Children need more than your presence these days.'
Tina, 37, civil servant

'He wishes he earned enough for both of us, but only because I would like to give up work. I do earn more than he does and it doesn't bother him at all. We have a joint account so there is no mine and yours as far as money is concerned.'
Tracey, 27, nanny/nursery nurse

'Yes, definitely. We have a good friend who earns more than her husband and mine is quite envious of him.'
Stephanie, 30, solicitor

'He's jealous and would not like it if I earned more than he did.'
Evelyn, 34, business information officer

'Yes, he would like it if I earned more. I think he'd retire and do something more interesting, although he's younger than I am.'
Carol, 43, self-employed business administrator

'I think he would feel embarrassed if I earned more than he did; he is a "professional" man!'
Lucy, 38, secretary/PA & research interviewer

'My partner feels inadequate at the moment. He probably would not mind me earning more if he were employed, but as I am the main earner, he's not happy.'

Jan, 43, hotel manager

'I have earned more than him and he was fine about it. All our money goes on childcare and food anyway.'

Judith, 36, chartered physiotherapist

'I do earn more and it doesn't make any difference. Our money is for our family and for our life together.'

Margaret, 47, senior medical laboratory scientific officer

'We are a partnership, so I don't think he would like me, as an equal, to earn more than him.'

Diane, 38, company director

'He copes with me earning more, although he doesn't like being reminded of it.'

Karen, 32, accountant

What proportion of your money goes on childcare/bills/food/children's clothes etc?

'I prefer to have my own bank account because it gives me a stronger sense of independence, Some 70 per cent of my money goes on childcare and bills etc. so I have about 30 per cent left to spend or save.'

Myra, 36, teacher of English as a foreign language

'Food: 25 per cent; bills: 25 per cent; children's clothes: 10 per cent. I don't have savings. I dress well so my spare money goes on clothes, shoes and holidays.'

Lynda, 41, marketing executive

'The money I earn is for food, the children and myself. My husband pays all the bills and childcare. I'd hope to contribute more in the future, when the children are older.'

Theresa, 37, teacher

'He pays for the food, clothes and household bills. I pay for luxuries only: furniture, car purchases and unusual things that we could do without if I didn't work. My salary is put into a "joint pot" as savings.'

Sue, 42, secretary

'We pool all our income so it's not my money. We are now in a position that I can spend money on myself and not feel guilty. I had none for myself when the children were under three.'

Pauline, 41, teacher

'Childcare/food/bills etc. takes care of 80 per cent. Edward was not planned (three bottles of wine and no condom!), so we were in debt when he was born, and still are.'

Jacqueline, 29, personnel officer/PA

'All my money goes on childcare and bills etc. I spend £10 per month on myself, and we have joint savings of £50 per month.'

Linda, 35, diocesan registry clerk

'None of my money goes on childcare etc. Currently it is all being re-invested in my business, being used for computer hardware, software, scanners etc. We manage on what my husband earns.'

Claire, 34, marketing consultant

'We share everything. If I want to buy something, I do, and the same goes for my husband. I think we have a marriage made in heaven. I was married before for thirteen years, which was hell.'

Irene, 42, hotelier

'One third of our joint £50,000 income goes on childcare/bills/food etc. We try to save £200 per month to spend on doing up our old house.'

Kathleen, 36, human resources adviser

How much do you get to spend on yourself, or save?

'I save £215 per month through share option schemes at work. I save £26 per month on an endowment for our child and about £35 per month on a similar endowment for ourselves – apart from the mortgage. We struggle the whole time and don't budget enough because we like too many luxuries. I hope it will be better next year when one of the share options is paid off.'

Audrey, 41, admin supervisor

'We pool everything, and then take £100 each per month as pocket money. Bills are paid from the pool.'

Deborah, 24, secretary

'We save nothing. Most months I spend next to nothing on myself. Once or twice a year I go clothes shopping, to the sale preview evenings at Debenhams, say, and then I put it all on my charge card in order to pay it off over the next few months. It is accepted that I manage our finances because I'm better at maths and work in a bank. However, it works better for us having separate bank accounts, so that we can each exercise some discretion in our spending.'

Carole, 36, bank manager

'I get £20 per month pocket money. Unbeknown to my husband, I am saving it – probably for a surprise romantic weekend. I've done it before.'

Susan, 37, WP operator/clerk

'I can't really say, but I do not go without, nor do I waste money. I would rather spend money on travelling and holidays than on shopping for the latest fashions each week. I have got nice clothes and shoes and I look after them so that they last longer.'

Sarah, 26, florist/student

'We don't see our earnings as something to be competitive about, as everything is all pooled in a joint account anyway. We save an agreed amount each month, which is deducted from my husband's salary. I spend quite a lot on clothes and have a Next account which I pay off every month (about £50).'

Elspeth, 38, teacher

'All our money goes into a joint account: we do not have my money and his money. I would spend up to about £100 without discussing it with my husband. Anything more than this and I would check we could afford it that month.'

Sarah, 36, research scientist

'Not enough. Unfortunately, I do like nice things. I don't get them – but I can dream! I have to put a lot of money back into my business. All my money disappears at the moment but that's because my business is still so young.'

Linda, 39, saddler

'I smoke so that's the money I spend on myself: £20 per month.'
Beverley, 28, civil servant

'As much as I want. But I'm not very interested in shopping, nor clothes, so I don't spend much really.'
Annie, 42, NHS chief executive

'I always treat myself to a facial and a leg wax each month. I keep my polo membership, visit Royal Ascot and spend quite a bit on make-up and glossy mags.'
Alexandra, 37, computer systems analyst

'Nothing to spend, nor to save. We have been chronically in debt since we've had children. At times it has been a strain on the relationship, and a considerable source of worry.'
Charlotte, 33, doctor, senior registrar level, training

'Most of my wages now goes on children's clothes, childcare, school holidays and little luxuries. I try to save a small amount each week and tend to buy clothes by mail order when I desperately need them, not just because I like them.'
Janet, 39, catering assistant

Tips

1. Have a plan and stick to it.

2. Let one partner manage the money. Talk about the needs for a particular month: birthdays, school uniforms, shoes, for example. Then work out your cash flow accordingly.

3. If you have a big freezer and enough storage space, shop monthly. You can save a lot of money that way.

4. Have your salaries paid into your own accounts, with a realistic proportion of each salary being transferred into a joint account for bills.

5. Pay all regular bills by direct debit. Pay on a monthly plan so that you know your monthly outgoings for all important bills.

6. Have one account for all bills including council tax, rates, car tax, insurance etc. and provide a fixed amount monthly (to cover total bills divided by twelve), thus ensuring that bills do not appear out of the blue.

7. Never overdraw. If you cannot afford it, go without.

8. Talk about where the money goes, so that no hidden resentment builds up.

9. Try not to worry too much. Keep things in proportion.

10. Use mail order when you can, it helps spread the cost.

11. Make credit cards work for you but do not overspend; it is an easy trap.

Family

'They don't take my career seriously.'

'Mummy, Sally's got a huge tummy, hasn't she?' Natalie observed, inches away from the aforementioned bulge, which looked even bigger than normal encased in a puce pink floral minidress.

'Yes, Natalie, she's got a little baby in there,' I said, relieved that Sally was pregnant and not just fat like the woman on the bus that Natalie had been staring at so fixedly the day before.

'The baby'll be coming out soon, won't he, Mummy, and we can see him then?'

'Yes, we will. Do you remember we talked about how your friend Amy will be a sister once the baby's been born?'

Long silence. . . .

'I haven't got a sister though, Mummy,' she said, sadly pulling at the hem of her dress, 'have I?'

Oh-oh, dodgy ground. Warning signs started flashing furiously before my eyes.

'I haven't got a brother either, have I?'

'No . . .' I hesitated, wondering what was the easiest way of getting out of this one.

'Never mind, Mummy,' she said, snuggling up close, suddenly happy again in the lightning way that only under-fives can manage, 'we've got each other.'

Happy family moments are best savoured and memorized to be replayed over and over again through the years to blot out the petty squabbles and teenage confrontations. We all hate the idea that history repeats itself and that we will turn into our mothers, having the same arguments with our children that we had with them. I hated mine saying: 'No, you can't do that, you'll understand why when you're older and have childen of your own.' I used to think that was a feeble argument because it seemed unlikely, if I couldn't understand then, that a few more years would make any difference at all? The maddening thing is that, of course, as soon as I had Natalie, I did understand and appreciated most of the things that my parents had done for me because I knew that they had acted out of love and concern for my welfare.

According to the women who contributed to this book, how your mother will feel about you combining work and family life very much depends on what she did. Some 65 per cent of their mothers worked while they were young – either full time or part time – and 67 per cent said that they received no pressure from their mothers to stay at home and bring their children up.

But when it came to how their partners' parents felt – the 'dreaded' in-law factor – there was nowhere near the same level of understanding: 26 per cent said their in-laws really did not like them working, or had not made their feelings clear. Only 13 per cent had voiced their wholehearted support.

What pressures are there from your parents to 'build a home' rather than a career?

'There are no pressures. They wish I had a proper career, because I went to grammar school and, in their eyes, wasted my education.'

Tracey, 27, nanny/nursery nurse

'I get pressure from my mother. I do too much, and she worries that I will be ill.'

Joy, 41, general assistant/business proprietor/care assistant

'My mother thinks that I should stay at home with the kids, even though she worked. My gran is horrified that I work. I've told my mother that I'll retire when I'm the Commissioner and not before.'

Carol, 33, police officer

'Their criticisms tend to take the form of sideways comments. I just have to ignore them and understand that everyone has their own opinion. My mother didn't work until I was in my teens.'

Donna, 30, registered nurse (for the mentally handicapped)

'None, my parents are supportive of whatever I do.'

Susan, 27, insurance clerk

'I am the only working mum in my family, and they make me feel like I should be at home looking after the kids.'

Mandy, 28, hairdresser

'They criticize any home inadequacies, like a messy bedroom or something like that, but are actually more critical of my attempts to have a social life without my daughter Emma.'

Maria, 33, accountant

'None. They realize that no one is going to support me. I think they quite admire me.'

Di, 30, quality control supervisor (food industry)

'I get a lot of pressure from them. The failure of my marriage has been put down partially to stresses caused by my working.

However, my parents do accept that I am in a better position now, without my ex-husband.'

Jenny, 27, systems analyst/IT manager

'They enjoy the reflected glory, but privately let me know that they think a mother should be at home.'

Judith, 36, chartered physiotherapist

'My parents are dead now, but they were always very concerned that until I was 33, I had a career rather than a husband or children. My mother didn't work; my father was completely against it.'

Jill, 39, university administrator

'I get no pressure from my family because they live 6,000 miles away. After the initial shock of me leaving my first husband and moving to another country to marry a disabled man fourteen years my senior, they've had nothing but support and encouragement for me and my endeavours.'

Sheila, 33, director/company secretary/ manufacturer of communication equipt. for people who cannot speak

'My mother is supportive but finds it difficult to understand my reasons for wanting to work. She didn't work when we were pre-school age.'

Louise, 35, freelance market research moderator

'My parents would have had a fit if I'd given up work after all the support they had given me through school and university.'

Sue, 36, deputy head teacher

'My father made it clear that he thought I should stay at home with the baby. He never really forced this view on me, though, and let me go my own way. Since then he has told my mother *that he thinks returning to work part time is working well for me and the baby.'*

Kathryn, 32, senior computer programmer/analyst

'None. My parents are extremely proud of my career and achievements. They also admit that my children are extremely well balanced, confident and happy.'

Moira, 36, business consultant/area manager

Prince's Youth Business Trust

'My mother took a long time to accept that I wanted to be a working mother. She still doesn't really agree but realizes that I couldn't stay at home all the time. She only worked part time herself when I was at school.'

Jackie, 32, practice nurse

'I get no pressure from them at all. My mother has always worked/juggled. I still don't know how she did it, because there were three of us. My father had a heart attack, and she ran a licensed guest house for six months with no staff!'

Beverley, 28, civil servant

'I'm very lucky with both sets of parents. They are all interested in what I do. My mother didn't work, but now she works for me.'

Gill, 32, owner/manager of children's day nursery

'My mother, sister and mother-in-law assumed that I would give up work when my first child came along – just as they all had. My mother gave me a hard time: I was doing everything wrong. It was "That poor boy needs more cuddles, and more time." My husband's parents now happily accept my work because they can see the children are happy and well.'

Brenda, 33, business development manager

'We informed them early that my husband would be the parent staying at home. I don't think they truly believed it until he did it.'

Joy, 36, teacher

'My dad is a real chauvinist. He doesn't believe in women working, and my mother agrees with everything he says. They don't take my career very seriously, and I detect an undercurrent of disapproval.'

Stephanie, 30, solicitor

'No pressures – I'm always "building homes" (nine so far in 12 years of marriage), so I'm getting good at it. But I also get very frustrated at times.'

Lindsay, 39, supply teacher (former WRAF personnel officer)

How do your partner's parents feel about you working?

'My mother-in-law (unfortunately and stereotypically) comes from hell. Anything I did would be wrong. She hates me because I am working class and younger than her son!'

Pat, 39, university lecturer

'My mother-in-law has never worked and is from a generation and class that has no conception of "work".'

Miranda, 39, manager of workplace nursery

'Initially she tried to talk me out of returning to work. Now she is fully supportive and helps with childcare.'

Karen, 32, insurance underwriter

'Whenever there was an accident, or if Rebecca got ill, I'd hear, "Well, it wouldn't have happened if she'd been with her mother."'

Frances, 38, personal assistant

'I have no pressures from my partner's parents. They know how necessary it is for me to work because of the maintenance he has to pay to his ex-wife and the negative equity situation we are in on a property we used to live in and currently rent out – but at a loss.'

Sue, 35, personnel manager

'My partner's parents cannot conceive of women having careers. They have no idea of how much I do; they think it is a nice little job to keep me out of mischief.'

Stephanie, 31, midwife

'My husband's mother feels that I should be at home with my son. She views my career as subservient to my husband's, and is worried about the effect my work is having on Alex and on our home life.'

Christine, 30, financial controller

'My partner's family and my mum are very encouraging and supportive, while my dad and step-father are disapproving. They don't nag me about it; they just avoid the subject.'

Sally, 24, library assistant

'Although my mother-in-law says she thinks it's admirable, I sense that she disapproves of the fact that I expect my partner to cook and clean and care for the kids as well. My father-in-law never did any housework, nor did he get involved in childcare. His traditional wife stayed at home, and even stirred his tea for him!'

Helen, 32, staff nurse/full-time student

'My in-laws totally disapprove of me working and don't talk to me.'

Helen, 38, solicitor

'My ex-husband's parents didn't mind if I took dead-end jobs, but seemed to think that any sort of demanding job was unsuitable.'

Jane, 25, housing officer

'While my family is very supportive, I get a lot of unhelpful comments and masses of disapproval from Frank's mother. She says the usual things like: "A mother's place is in the home." Although she works now, she didn't until her youngest was five – and that was part-time night shifts. My in-laws also disapprove of Frank's involvement in childcare and household chores.'

Isobel, 31, psychiatric ward sister

'They seem to think that it is a good thing that I work because I contribute to the financial areas of our relationship and relieve some of the pressure on my husband.'

Tracey, 31, sensory analyst

'As a Catholic materfamilias, my mother-in-law thought it was disgusting and never lost an opportunity to make her feelings plain.'

Fiona, 40, health visitor

How does the fact that you have a career and children compare with your siblings' lives?

'It's vastly different. My sister "had to marry", became a single parent, re-married and has never had the holidays abroad, business lunches etc. that I enjoy. She does, however, have an enviable relationship with her daughters.'

Dianne, 40, civil servant

'My sister can't have children and has retired early from the police force. She is 39 years old and now has an active life and doesn't regret a thing. I envy her sometimes. My 35-year-old brother has five children. His wife childminds and at times they find it hard.'

Susan, 37, WP operator/clerk

'My sister and two sister-in-laws stay at home with their children. Sometimes I think they are envious because my life doesn't revolve totally around the children.'

Mary, 56, customer services manager

'I am the only member of my family of six children to have a career, and the only one of the four girls to work while my children were tiny.'

Jill, 39, university administrator

'My sister and her family are very different to us. Her attitude is that I was always the one who would make something of my life. She worked very successfully in a bank for many years and now, with two children, works as a teacher's assistant at her son's school. We have very different aspirations, but there is no jealousy on either part. They are a solid couple; people who wouldn't take a gamble. We are just the opposite; we think of an idea and make it happen. The insecurity of our lifestyle would probably worry them to death.'

Lyn, 42, picture framer/overseas demonstrator

'They have no kids and spend all their money on themselves. I miss that sometimes.'

Margaret, 23, part-time bank official/fitness instructor

'My sister stays at home, but she's broke and sad. I love her dearly, but she can't help herself.'

Jill, 34, university technician/owner of security business

'My sister married young and had her first child when she was 20. Now all the children are grown up, she has trained for and has a successful career. I think we both envied each other during our 20s, but for different reasons. I had my freedom and fun, but lacked goals or direction. My sister had a fulfilling family life and was still young enough to start her career in her early 30s. I would have preferred to have started my family when I was younger.'

Judy, 37, lecturer/musician

'I was the first in the family to combine the two and I did worry at first about whether I would be able to cope. My sister and sister-in-law are full-time mums but I don't think I manage worse or do any less for our daughter than they do for their kids.'

Alexandra, 37, computer systems analyst

'My sister is married with a career and no children, so my life is much busier. She socializes more and plays golf!'

Gillian, 48, accounts manager

'My brother's wife earns more than he does in a high-pressure career. He does a lot of childcare, but they love each other. My ex-husband hated the fact that I had a career and earned more. That is the difference.'

Joanna, 43, casualty nurse

'My sister has always preferred not to work since having a child, regardless of the fact that she was highly qualified in her previous career.'

Sylvia, 40, fee earner (solicitors)/founder member
of Support and Survival

'I have two sisters; they both have families. One works and her children are very happy. My brothers' wives all work. The sister who does not work has three, very noisy, unruly boys, who are not particularly sociable.'

Moira, 36, business consultant/area manager Prince's Youth
Business Trust

'Sometimes I envy my sisters who stay at home with their children.'

Bushra, 43, community staff nurse/part-time staff nurse

'Very different. They had jobs as an extra interest or to earn pin money; my salary is essential, and I have a far more demanding job.'

Janet, 39, commercial manager of professional football club

Tips for dealing with family criticism

1. Make sure first that it's real and not imagined. Some people think their parents might disapprove when actually they don't.

2. Don't apologize for your lifestyle. Stand firm and politely assert your views. Be open to discussion but remember that only you can decide what is best for your family.

3. Make it clear why you work and show them how enthusiastic you are about it.

4. Be strong and confident because if you are happy, the children will be too, and your family will see that mixing careers and families does not result in maladjusted, emotionally deprived children.

5. Work out who is being critical and whether they know enough about your needs for their opinion to be valuable.

6. Involve your family in discussions about activities you undertake with the children. Emphasize positive points. Visit grandparents regularly.

7. Understand that different generations have different values and attitudes.

8. If you have to work for financial reasons and your relations are still critical, ask them to pay your mortgage.

Friends

'They keep me sane.'

We are born into our families, but we can choose our friends. So, if we are not getting the love and support from our relations that we need to cope with our over-burdened lives, then having friends who are going through it all too can be a wonderful comfort and source of advice and inspiration – as long as they are willing to share their expertise with us, that is.

I have been known to flick through the parenting/child health reference books – usually to back up my mother's intuition in the small hours before calling out the doctor – but when it comes to the nitty gritties of teething problems, potty training and foot-stamping tantrums, nothing beats a reassuring chat with my best friends. Very few of those with children work full time, but they are completely supportive and have never made me feel guilty.

If your friends are making you feel inadequate by harping on about how much they do with their children, or gloating about how advanced young Tommy is – *'He was completely dry by the time he was 18 months, you know. It's a shame your Emma's still in nappies isn't it? Still it's only to be expected with the busy life you lead.'* – then stop seeing them, if they are upsetting you, or emphasize how sociable and independent your children are.

More than half the women surveyed said that most of their friends with children worked, and only six per cent said that their friends thought their children were missing out because they worked.

Do most of your friends with children work? If not, how supportive are they?

'I was the first of my friends to work full time with small children, and most of them seemed to think I was mad. However, now, one by one, all but a few seem to have returned to some form of work.'

Wendy, 36, beauty therapist

'No, they don't, and I don't think that they have any idea how hard it can be. They talk about a busy week when they have to fit in a haircut and a visit from the gas man!'

Sue, 36, deputy head teacher

'I think the ones who don't work pity my situation and wouldn't dare not be supportive, even if it's not how they would raise their own kids.'

Jane, 35, public relations/marketing manager

'I sometimes feel guilty when I see their tidy homes, their home baking and the pictures etc. that have resulted from playing with their children and so on.'

Joanna, 37, local government officer

'They do not make me feel guilty. They accept me as I am, and I accept them as they are. The world is made interesting by differences. And we all have our children's welfare at heart.'

Margaret, 47, senior medical laboratory scientific officer

'No, they don't work and they often make me feel guilty. They say that I'm not with my children enough, and that I'm tired and they ask me why I had children at all.'

Nicola, 34, air-traffic controller

'Some of my friends think that it's odd that I chose to work, because we don't actually "need" me to.'

Valerie, 33, part-time special needs assistant

'No, most of my friends don't work and those that do, work part time. They tend to admire me and say things like "God, I don't know how you do it, you must have so much energy" etc..'

Allyson, 33, teacher/head of department

'It's more or less half and half. People try desperately to be forward-thinking and modern, but most have an inbuilt basic disapproval of working mums. I get funny looks and feel that I have to apologize for working.'

Donna, 30, registered nurse (for the mentally handicapped)

'Some work and some don't. It is not difficult to make me feel guilty about the time I don't spend with my children, though. I have a predisposition to guilt: I am a woman.'

Claire, 36, social worker

'Non-working friends have made comments about feeling that it's not fair to leave their children when they're still so young, that it's such a short time etc. I point out how being exposed to other adults results in confident and adaptable children; how well they relate to people; how much attention they get from their minder, who concentrates on them, rather than doing the housework.'

Elspeth, 38, teacher

'Yes, most work, but many are part time or job share. Most are very supportive; we cover for one another on the odd occasion when the children are ill.'

Stephanie, 31, midwife

'Half of them work and half don't. The ones who don't are mostly supportive. They don't make me feel guilty, but often they can't understand that its not the money that motivates me.'

Janey, 35, chartered quantity surveyor

'I have found myself making friends and keeping in touch with people who do work and have kids, as we share similar ideas; they keep me sane. I don't quite fit in with the friends I have locally any more because they're all full-time mothers.'

Nikki, 34, TV producer/journalist

'Most who don't work at all make me feel guilty; not through their attitudes, but because they are always so organized. I feel like my children and I are barely holding it together sometimes.'

Sarah, 37, college lecturer (fashion design)

'I had children earlier than any of my friends. Many of them regard me as a role model now that I have three. I am no expert but can advise people going through it all for the first time – although most of the time you don't feel you are doing well enough. What keeps you sane is having one or two female friends who are close enough for you to be able to offload all the bad bits onto.'

Charlotte, 33, doctor/senior registrar

'They never make me feel guilty. They respect my decision. Sometimes they do forget that I work full time when making social arrangements.'

Gillian, 35, systems training designer

'My 20-year-old daughter is the only one who really makes me bristle; she doesn't work and spends a lot of time with her daughter. I have had a lot of flack because my two-year-old still has her dummy. Frankly, my 20-year-old daughter sucked her

thumb and, in fact, still does when she watches television. I can throw away the dummy in time.'
Lindsey, 38, school secretary

'Interestingly, the wife of one of my cousins said she didn't approve of my working, but now she has had two children of her own in quick succession and says she wishes that she could get a job!'
Diane, 29, insurance underwriter

'Half my friends with children work. They are all supportive. We have each other's children to stay from time to time so that everyone gets a night without them – excellent!'
Jane, 33, local government manager

'My neighbour has a child the same age as Molly. She tries to agree that nursery is a good idea, but she manages to make me feel guilty too, somehow.'
Sarah, 28, regional administrative officer

'My friends who don't work do not understand how hectic life becomes with a job as well. They cannot see why you haven't time for coffee on a non-work day.'
Helen, 27, agricultural consultant

'I think the ones who don't work envy me – but I envy them!'
Jayne, 38, estate agent

Tips for handling competitive, full-time mums

1. Relax and be confident in your parenting abilities. Your children will grow up with a broader base of experience and you'll be better able to provide for them financially.

2. Remember that no one is perfect – including full-time mums! We are all different; it is not a question of better or worse.

3. They seem to think that you have the best of both worlds. In fact, you do not have the best of either: you do not know other mothers at school and you cannot socialize with colleagues from work.

4. Stress the individuality of children and mothers, and children's adaptibility to situations, and the need to be flexible to make things work.

5. Tell full-time mums that they're marvellous because it's one of the hardest jobs in the world.

6. Remember: every child is different and will reach the milestones like potty training when they are good and ready. It has nothing to do with whether their mother works or not.

7. There's bound to be something your child is better at doing. Focus on it, if you have to, to make yourself feel better.

8. Make friends with working mums at work.

9. Smile sweetly and walk away.

999

'I panic and phone my mother.'

'It's *dangerous to run in the road, isn't it, Mummy?'* Natalie said, watching a little boy outside a school being told off by his parents for doing just that.

'Yes,' I said, pleased that she had obviously remembered what I had told her some weeks before. '*Some cars are very fast and if a little boy or girl runs out in front of them, they might not be able to stop in time – so you must stay on the pavement or hold hands with Mummy or Daddy when we cross the road.'*

'*The car could run me down otherwise, couldn't it? Would I be crying, Mummy?'*

'*Yes, you would, and so would Mummy and Daddy. It's not a good game to play – it's far too painful . . .'* I paused trying to think of a good example of how painful it might be, without scaring her too much '. . . *remember when you cut your knee?'*

'*Uhuh.'*

'*Well, it would hurt much, much more than that and even more than the time you fell off the bed and banged your head.'*

'*Really?'* she said, in what sounded suspiciously like an excited tone. '*I'd have to go to the hospital then. I like the hospital; they had a Christmas tree there. And I'd have to take medicine. Medicine tastes nice. . . .'*

It's fine to sit down to watch *Casualty*, *ER* and *Medics*, because no matter how real the situations appear, we know that it is only television. We can, however, do without that kind of excitement in real life.

It is only when an emergency strikes that we find out whether we are generally managing to hold all the various sections of our life together, or whether we are daily teetering on the brink of disaster. If our support mechanisms are strong, then with any luck, like the foundations of our homes, we should still be standing when the storm has subsided.

Most of the women to whom I spoke said that when they were ill, they tended to struggle on regardless, but when their child or carer was bedridden, the alarm bells started to ring and partners/family/friends were drafted in to help. If the illness was serious, then employers had to be told. But would they always get the whole truth? For 60 per cent of the women honesty was the only way. They said they always told their employer they had to take time off to look after a sick child; only six per cent admitted to lying and saying that they were ill themselves instead.

So how do employers normally react? Just under and just over a quarter said their bosses were very understanding and 'okay' about it respectively. Just three per cent hated the inconvenience.

How do you cope when you/your child/ your child's carer is ill?

'If I am ill, I keep working unless I'm dying (not literally). I have an excellent family who would help me if Charlotte was ill. The nursery has plenty of staff so I never have to worry. If any of them are ill, they have cover.'

Karen, 28, caterer

'I feel as the company is paying me to work seven hours a day for so many days in the year, that it is up to me to be there, unless I am genuinely ill; I take any other time off as holidays, or possibly unpaid. It is not the company's responsibility that I have a child, although I would expect them to show compassion in a real emergency, as I hope they would if it was a partner or parent who was ill.'

Audrey, 41, admin supervisor

'I always have a back-up organized. I have never needed to take time off because of child illness.'

Sue, 35, training manager

'If I'm ill, I struggle to cook and look after Emma as usual I save annual leave for when Emma or my carer is ill, and use flexi-time or other help.'

Maria, 33, accountant

'If I am ill, my mother or my husband looks after the children. When Jennifer broke her leg badly last year, and had to stay home for two months, my mother and I staggered the childcare. When my father was ill last summer, I decided to find a nursery for James because up until then Mum had looked after him, and when Mum was ill this year, I looked after my Dad while she was in hospital. I am now busy making up my lost working hours!'

Joanna, 37, local government officer

'If my children are ill Sunday to Friday, I look after them. If they are ill on a Saturday (however bad they are) my parents have to take over. I get booked up to take wedding photographs up to two years in advance, so I cannot and don't let people down.'

Pam, 32, wedding photographer

'On one occasion, when my son was ill, I took him in the car with me to visit my patients. He forgot he was ill and enjoyed himself enormously because all the elderly made a fuss of him.'

Bushra, 43, community staff nurse/part-time staff nurse

'In the past I've not gone to work. For long-term illness, my parents came 200 miles to care for my youngest. The conflict between being a good mother and working full time does get me down when the children are ill. I have sent my son to school with tonsillitis, because I thought he only had a cold; I felt rotten afterwards when I realized what was really wrong with him. I have also taken a day off and he has seemed fine by 9.30 am!'

Denise, 39, teacher

'My husband and I try to share the responsibility of having to take days off when Ben is ill. When he or I are ill, we look after each other. Luckily the nursery is never ill!'

Tracey, 31, sensory analyst

'I stay at home and pretend that I'm ill, or my partner stays at home.'

Patricia, 39, operating theatre sister

'I panic and phone my mother. I don't think I'll ever get used to this!'

Tracey, 31, social worker

'If I were ill, my husband or parents would help. If my children are ill, I miss university and work. I just can't bear to leave them with anyone else. At university it doesn't matter, but you have to catch up – they never let you off work. At the nursing home you're expected to try and find someone to cover for you.'

Helen, 32, staff nurse/full-time student

'When I'm ill, I go to bed; I don't believe in struggling on – it'll only get worse. In a way it is quite good because it's the only time that I get a break from work and childcare. If my child is ill, my husband and I do shifts. Fortunately, his work is quite flexible. If my carer is ill, my mother-in-law helps out or we do shifts as before. My employer is resentful and gets exasperated if I need time off.'

Victoria, 34, chartered accountant

'I've been lucky. I've only had one illness in the family. I just rushed off without explaining and nobody missed me! Sad really.'

Janette, 30, senior systems analyst

'I call on my mother in an emergency. My employer reacts very well, but his children are exactly the same age so he's very understanding.'

Caroline, 31, corporate PR manager

'I used to phone around my friends frantically when I needed help with my first baby, but now I put the children first every time.'

Jayne, 38, estate agent

What do you tell your employer if you need time off?

'It depends, my job is very flexible – so sometimes I'm honest and sometimes I don't tell. I do believe, though, that it's better to be frank. Motherhood is something to be proud of, and an employer can consider having priorities responsible.'

Julie, 30, business manager

'If the children are ill, I have to ring in and say that I am sick or take unpaid leave/holiday. No allowance is made for sick children in the NHS.'

Joanna, 43, casualty nurse

'I take time off immediately and then negotiate time in lieu or special leave with my boss at a later date. I tell the truth – but I invest in the service. I provide a high level of quality and commitment, so expect understanding and support if I need leave.'

Judith, 36, chartered physiotherapist

'I tell my employer the truth and have to take the time off out of my annual holiday entitlement.'

Di, 30, quality control supervisor (Food Industry)

'I've been honest in the past, explaining that my childminder is ill. This was not treated sympathetically, so next time I will say that I'm ill.'

Alison, 37, senior registrar (Obstetrics & Gynaecology)

'I tell the truth: my family comes before my job. When I had a female boss, she was very difficult – she had employed a full-time nanny. My male boss was very understanding, and would stand in for me himself.'

Carol, 45, teacher

'When I was honest, I was docked a day's pay, so now I lie and say I am ill.'

Sarah, 37, college lecturer

'My employers react very well. One has children of his own, and the other doesn't but appreciates honesty, i.e., that I don't ring in sick myself.'

Sarah, 28, regional administrative officer

'I tell my employer the truth, because we have a good special leave procedure.'

Marcia, 35, Royal Mail collections manager

'There are three of us who work together and all have young children. We cover for each other. Any overtime incurred by covering is taken as time back. My immediate manager is quite understanding if I need time off, providing that we organize cover between ourselves.'

Jackie, 32, practice nurse

What is the worst situation you have found yourself in at work?

'My mother-in-law crashed the car and I got a call about it at work, in the middle of an important meeting. I dropped everything and rushed home.'

Catherine, 39, senior secretary

'Louis being sick in our gift shop in front of two customers. Louis hiding my car keys in a filing cabinet while my back was turned, so I had to beg for a lift home and spent the whole day the next day searching for them.'

Angela, 35, buyer (for a charity)

'Having a serious business meeting while my two-year-old son had a tantrum with his father outside the office door – terrible!'

Ann, 41, chartered accountant

'I am about to embark upon it: my mother-in-law (chief helper) is about to go into hospital for two new knee replacements. The following month my senior therapist goes on holiday for three weeks and one of my junior therapists is leaving and as yet I have not found a suitable replacement. My salon is open 9 am to 9 pm seven days a week and I will be on my own.'

Wendy, 36, beauty therapist

'Between childminders I had to bring my two-month-old baby in to work with me. It was a nightmare. I even changed her nappy on the conference room table and she had to attend a meeting with me. NEVER AGAIN!'

Jane, 35, PR/marketing manager

'Coping with the trauma of divorce and having to continue to work, as well as bringing up a child.'

Lesley, 40, photographer/book-keeper

'Having to try to get home when there wasn't a train for five hours. When I told my boss, and bearing in mind that it was the first time this had happened in five years, all he said was: "What are you going to do about making up the lost time?" I was fuming. Luckily, another colleague drove me 10 miles to the next station, and I'd already put in more than sufficient hours at that stage.'

Di, 30, quality control supervisor

'When I phoned home and my 12- and 14-year-old sons were fighting because one had hurt the pet mice while they were racing them. My friend gave them the train fare and they met me at work.'

Claire, 36, social worker

'When my ex-husband walked out with no notice after 10½ years. I got home from my day job at 2 pm to find a note to say that he'd gone into town, so I had to cancel my night work and my boss wasn't very pleased. I didn't know how long my

husband would be gone; in fact, he never came back. I tracked him down three days later. He had just turned up on his ex-girlfriend's doorstep and she had taken him in!'
Caroline, 35, take-away manager

'*Being in the middle of a complex medical procedure that I can't leave and being bleeped by someone telling me that Cassie is unwell: I got a phone call at 2 am from my husband saying Cassie was ill and I was in the process of delivering a still birth. The sister in charge was an unsympathetic (single) older woman.'*
Stephanie, 31, midwife

'*Having three hours sleep and doing a major presentation.'*
Caroline, 31, corporate PR manager

'*Emma was born on the day we had a wedding. I went into labour at 8 am on the Saturday morning and we went to the hospital and called the community midwife. Fortunately, my labours are nice and quick and Emma was born at 11.40 am – just in time for me to have a shower before Roy had to go in order to get to the bride's home for 1 pm. If Emma hadn't made it before midday, Roy would have left me and my best friend would have taken over. I would have felt very guilty if Roy had missed the birth as it was very important for him to be there for all three. I accepted the booking as I was convinced that Emma was not going to be born on a Saturday afternoon. She made it. Roy picked me up at 5 pm the same day and we went home to be with the boys.'*
Pam, 32, wedding photographer

'*I once took my daughter to work with me and she became ill. My husband was at work and could not be contacted; my mother was away. I couldn't close the kennels until 6 pm because I was working on my own, and had lots of dogs and cats to clean out,* exercise, feed, and a sick three-year-old to look after in the middle of winter, outside in the cold. Not easy.'

Caroline, 32, kennels & cattery proprietor

'My 14-year-old son was alone at home and telephoned me at work in tears, feeling really ill. I was a two-hour journey away.'

Deborah, 36, freelance journalist

'Being in court giving evidence on behalf of a client and being handed a note by the usher saying that my child had been admitted to hospital. I read the note, explained that I had a very serious personal domestic crisis and asked if the court would please ask me any relevant questions immediately or ask for an adjournment, if they felt it more appropriate. The court was sympathetic.'

Charlotte, 50, probation officer

'All three of my children got chickenpox, one after the other! And I had to stay at home.'

Karen, 35, video editor/student

My three-year-old shut his fingers in a fire door. I was told that if the office was left unmanned, I would be fired. I had to wait for someone to cover for me until I could go to the hospital.'

Jayne, 38, estate agent

'It's not the emergencies that give me problems. It's the "grey-area situations" like Alex being away on business, the kids being bored at home, the in-laws wanting a break and a deadline looming. Do I hang the deadline, take some leave and take the children and the in-laws to the seaside? Or do I press on, facing the children's complaints daily and the in-laws' moans, all on my own?'

Kwen, 35, psychologist

Tips for dealing with emergencies

1. DON'T PANIC!
2. Make a list of people (with their consent) who can and will help in an emergency and keep their numbers with you at all times.
3. Have contingency plans. If you don't shirk at other times, you might find your employer more willing to be helpful.
4. Try to lessen the effects of emergencies by working near home or having a standby carer if possible.
5. Be honest and professional but do not feel guilty. Your colleagues all have emergencies at some time or another.
6. Don't be afraid to ask for help from family/ friends/ workmates.
7. Children are stronger than you give them credit for. Explain what is going on.
8. Try to keep a week's holiday available to be taken at short notice.
9. Remember that no one is indispensable at work, but you're the only mother that your child has.
10. When the dust has settled, down a stiff drink!

Relaxation

'A curry, a bottle of wine and my husband.'

After you have read this chapter, lock yourself away somewhere on your own – the bathroom will do fine. Close your eyes for 15 minutes and escape into your very own world of relaxation. Where will you be? On a white sand beach watching the waves lapping against the shore? In a cornfield swaying with the breeze? Or gently floating down to earth – your colourful parachute billowing out above you?

Wherever you have been, you will feel refreshed and ready to enter the household/work fray again – yes, really. Of course, it's not the same as in the years BC (Before Children) when you might spend the whole of Sunday relaxing, but even 15 minutes spent totally relaxing your mind and body is better than none at all. So, to the 12 per cent of women polled who said they never had a chance to relax, give it a go and see if it helps.

Of the 32 per cent of women who admitted that they actively made time to relax, nearly a quarter unwound by reading. Going to the gym, swimming and other sports, having a long soak in the bath, and seeing friends were the next most popular ways to relax.

Do you get regular opportunities to relax? If so, what do you do?

'I have a horse and compete in show jumping competitions. Although this is tiring, it takes my mind off any problems and helps me relax.'

Karen, 28, caterer

'Relax – what's that? My ideas have changed rather. Now if I manage to sit for half an hour with a cup of coffee and a magazine, while the children are in bed, that's realxing.'

Tracey, 31, social worker

'I read every day, have a facial at the beauty salon every month, and I never work at the weekends because we always do something nice as a family.'

Ann, 41, chartered accountant

'No, I don't get regular opportunities to relax – I'm always uptight and tired. My jaw is permanently locked because of stress.'

Sheelagh, 33, accountant

'Yes, I paint picures. I go away once a year on a painting weekend. I swim occasionally, have a sunbed session and a massage and manicure regularly.'

Lynda, 41, marketing executive

'Not really, I would like to go to aerobics or swim, but my eldest child does things most evenings and my husband grizzles at being left to cope with collecting and bedtime.'

Susan, 42, biomedical scientist (microbiology)

'I go late-night shopping if in the mood, or just go out with a friend.'

Pauline, 31, paediatric endocrine nurse specialist

'I enjoy a sauna. I like a long bath with my She or Cosmo, or sit with my feet in the foot massager.'

Irene, 42, hotelier

'Not really. I'm quite happy with my busy week, although I do get very tired and look forward to weekends. I don't have much of a social life but it doesn't bother me as much as some of my friends seem to think it should.'

Patricia, 37, teaching assistant

'Yes. Aromatherapy massage once a month. Country walks with local group, and with friends most weekends. I like pottering about in the garden after Jason has gone to bed.'

Judy, 39, customer service officer

'Yes, I am very clear in my belief that life is to be enjoyed. I meet friends, do things with the children and swim.'

Annie, 42, NHS chief executive

'I go to mass. Church has become increasingly important to me. I take the kids; they are "trained" to behave.'

Pat, 39, university lecturer

'I read and walk the dog if I'm not too tired. Occasionally, I'll see friends and go to the theatre. I also sleep and my husband looks after our child then.'

Audrey, 41, admin supervisor

'I make time for myself – sometimes at the expense of other things. I socialize with my partner and friends a couple of

evenings each week. I like to have time to do a variety of things
– gardening, weight training, swimming, reading and writing
amongst them. I run a self-help group for victims of domestic
abuse: we meet every Wednesday and work through an
educational programme. I always feel a real lift when I leave
the group – and the others say they do too. The work we do is
really rewarding.'

Sylvia, 40, fee earner (solicitor)

'I don't get many opportunities to relax. I have one night where
I spoil myself – bath, face mask, body oil, early night.'

Lorraine, 32, intelligence analyst

'I keep Dexter cattle. Hand-milking is "me" time and I find it
very relaxing.'

Genevieve, 39, NHS administrator

'I rarely get opportunities to relax. Once or twice a year I will
get together with my best friend – another working mother –
and we go away for a few days to a health club or retreat.'

Cynthia, 40, managing director

'No. It's sitting or ironing in front of the television usually!'

Lucy, 38, secretary/PA & research interviewer

'I like doing my nails. It makes me feel good if I have nice hands.'

Coralie, 23, personal assistant

'I relax at work!'

Sarah, 28, regional administrative officer

'Meeting a male friend once a week for a drink; it makes me
feel like a woman rather than a wife/mother.'

Julie, 31, careers adviser

'Aromatherapy relaxes me. Putting calming oils on a tissue under my pillowcase at night, and relating the lovely smell to peace and sleep.'

Tessa, 42, physiotherapist/aromatherapist

'No, I don't get regular opportunities to relax – only occasional long baths. I have just had a week's holiday without my husband or child, which was wonderfully relaxing.'

Nicola, 29, antique furniture restorer

What is the happiest moment in your day/week?

'Friday evening with a curry, a bottle of wine, and my husband.'

Judy, 36, guidance officer/secretary

'When I come home from work and my son Josh runs up and hugs my legs with all his might.'

Catherine, 28, branch administrator

'Leaving the office and getting into the car – out of one world (of work) and not yet into the next (children and home).'

Joanna, 37, local government officer

'The happiest moment is a dinner by candlelight with my husband – much as we love our children.'

Donna, 41, receptionist

'I'm happy when my hour's workout in the gym is finished and I'm sitting in the steam room. I am also happy when we can relax as a family together.'

Susan, 37, WP operator/clerk

'Friday nights are the happiest. The thought of spending the whole weekend catching up with my daughter (and the laundry!) really puts me on a high.'

Jane, 35, PR/marketing manager

'Any time spent in absolute peace and quiet with no demands from anyone.'

Rebecca, 26, admin assistant

'The happiest moment I can think of is when my child is playing well and happily with his friends and I can talk to mine.'

Anne, 33, computer project manager

'Saturday evening when the children are in bed and I'm watching the National Lottery draw, drinking a glass of wine with my husband and dreaming of what I'd do with the million.'

Anne Marie, 31, part-time sales assistant

'When I eventually get into a nice cosy bed and cuddle up to my son Martin.'

Sarah, 26, florist/student

'My happiest moments are going to work when the kids are being horrid, and finishing work when the kids are being nice!'

Janice, 37, midwife

'Six o'clock in the morning in the fields with two happy golden retrievers running by my side. I walk with my dogs morning, evening and most weekends.'

Toni, 39, NHS senior manager

'Happiest moment is lying on the bed with my children's arms around me.'

Lorraine, 32, intelligence analyst

'Wednesday morning. I never go to the office and there's no one at home. I do exactly as I wish.'

Elizabeth, 51, fine art journal editor

'Saturday evenings, and being able to wake up naturally the next morning without an alarm.'

Jill, 40, sales coordinator

'Weekends: all in bed on a Saturday morning with toast, coffee, books, cuddles, being silly and laughing.'

Joy, 36, teacher

'When my boyfriend stays and I feel "normal" again.'

Yvonne, 38, research assistant (pharmology)/
Techno-Science & IT technician

'I love Saturday mornings when Sara fetches me breakfast in bed. Although it's usually something pretty inedible, it's lovely of her and we have half an hour together, talking.'

Julie, 35, hand embroiderer

'Bedtime. I sit and write in my journal and think about what I'm feeling. If it's bad, I wonder why, and what I can do about it. If I'm happy, I let myself really feel it.'

Gabrielle, 41, homeopath/counsellor

Tips for dealing with stress

1. Sit down and analyse whether the problem is really important. Prioritize your worries and deal with them individually.

2. Remove the item(s) causing stress: do the job you have been putting off, for example. Put things away properly: not finding things is stressful.

3. Talk over worries with your partner or a close friend.

4. Get plenty of fresh air. Get out of the house on your own and walk, breathe deeply or work out.

5. Don't take too much on, either at work or at home. The kids don't need entertainment twenty-four hours a day. They'll happily play in the garden instead of going out somewhere.

6. Make time each day to relax, even if it's just a long soak in the bath.

7. Have an all-over massage followed by very slow sex.

8. Indulge yourself. Use lunch breaks for yourself – go out alone rather than lunching with colleagues, or swim, or do a yoga class.

9. Work out what is valuable to you and what your needs are. Prune out the dead wood.

10. Don't give 100 per cent of yourself to your career and, if you can, pay someone to clean the house.

11. Set your goals to fit your lifestyle. Establish a routine to do certain things at certain times: hoover the living room, for example, on Thursdays, and clean the kitchen on Fridays. Stick to that, and don't worry about those jobs for the week in between, because you know they'll get done in due course.

12. Constantly give yourself positive messages about what you have achieved, no matter how small.

13. Work hard at maintaining a close circle of friends with and without children, and build a female support network.

14. Laughter is the best tonic in the world.

15. Go somewhere and have a good shout. Don't bottle it up inside.

16. If walls are closing in, find a gentle distraction: shopping, cinema, eating out, a holiday.

17. Do a stress management course.

18. Listen to a meditation tape.

19. Have a good session at the bottle bank!

20. Admit that you're tired; it is not a sign of weakness to ask for help.

21. Remember that some stress is healthy.

Attitudes

'I scream and have hysterics – then get on with it.'

'Mummy, are you a good girl?'

'Yes, Natalie, most of the time.'

'Mummy, am I a good girl?'

'Well, sometimes you are and sometimes you're naughty, aren't you?'

'Yes, Mummy, you're right,' she admitted pensively. 'Sometimes we're very bad girls, aren't we? Sometimes we shout at Daddy.'

'That's true,' I conceded, thankful that we were having this conversation at home and not in the supermarket queue.

'And sometimes,' she continued, warming to her theme, 'Daddy's a bad boy too when he shouts at us.'

Sometimes, when we eventually close our eyes to try to relax, thoughts creep into our heads that we have no time to deal with in our action-packed on-duty moments. 'Psst,' they whisper, *'are you really happy working so hard?'* When you try to think of your deserted beach or tranquil meadow and do not answer, they persist: *'But are your children happy?'*

'Yes,' you snap, trying to push your mental barriers into place to lock out those nagging voices, *'they're very happy, thank you.'* But they sneak in again through the cracks.

'Mrs So-and-so doesn't think they are. And you don't really do as much with them as you'd like do you?'

What other people think of us really does not matter; they are not an authority on our lives. But what we think of ourselves does. Nearly a quarter of the women to whom I spoke said that they felt they had sacrificed more in their lives by having a career, missing their children growing up and losing out on leisure time, but that they did not mind because their children were happy and benefited materially. The rest were evenly split between feeling angry that they had sacrificed too much, saying that they had a perfect balance between motherhood and their careers, and being convinced that they had sacrificed less by working.

As to feeling guilty about doing neither job well, 38 per cent said: 'No way!', while a quarter said: 'Of course we do!' and the remainder felt guilty sometimes or very rarely, depending on daily events and outside criticism of their mothering abilities (levelled at 27 per cent of them). Nearly half the women said that they were sorry they had to opt out of things they would like to do: becoming more involved with their children's school or playgroup, for example. But a fifth thought that they had more than enough to keep them occupied.

Weekends are supposed to be fun, aren't they? Well, one in 10 of the women polled said that they never think 'Thank God it's Friday.' They confess that they dread the weekends, preferring their weekly routines, while 33 per cent enjoy all seven days equally!

Do you feel you have sacrificed more or less by having a career?

'I have little time for myself, but the children are only young and so demanding for a short time. I plan to take up other hobbies when they are older.'

Anita, 35, software engineer

'I think I have sacrificed less personally, but as it contributed to my divorce, my son has to cope with a lot. However, now that I have graduated with a first-class degree, he sees me as something of a "role model".'

Sheila, 31, guidance development assistant/part-time student

'I feel I've got everything, a great job, wonderful family, but often I am so tired I can hardly speak. I need another few hours in the day.'

Karen, 28, caterer

'I don't have much time for myself, but am a 100 per cent better person for going out to work to when I stayed at home. Someone once said that children are a gift, and you should give up everything for them. They didn't have children.'

Michele, 31, secretary

'I don't feel I am a bad mother by working, but I feel I have hindered my career prospects by having a baby. Although I don't feel I do my job badly, because I'm a part-timer. I don't feel able to give it my all: keeping up with the law, for example, reading important journals and periodicals. I don't feel very marketable now, although I've never had a problem finding a job yet.'

Stephanie, 30, solicitor

'Even if I didn't work, I wouldn't have any time for myself. All three of my children need very little sleep, so there is very little time during or at the end of the day.'

Joanna, 37, local government officer

'Without my career, I would not have had the independence or guts to end my marriage.'

Denise, 39, teacher

'Definitely sacrificed less. I am "me" for five days a week and get social interaction. Otherwise I would find it difficult with a special needs child. My work time is to an extent my time and Sam benefits from his own social interaction and specialist care.'

Jenny, 27, systems analyst/IT manager

'I've sacrificed more. Life as a "kept" woman by a kind man would be lovely, but unfortunately many men use a wife's inferior job or lack of it as a chance to dominate and scorn. I have respect and freedom.'

Maria, 33, accountant

'I have not sacrificed anything except during the first two years with each child when I did not go out much (with friends) in the evenings (keep fit etc.)'

Margaret, 47, senior medical laboratory scientific officer

'Unfortunately, you can't have everything. Work has undoubtedly helped me to develop as a person, given me wider horizons and independence – and I do think this helps in my role as a mother. But the maternal feeling that I should be "around" more doesn't go away, and most of my other time is spent on family. Now I do try to do some things for myself: aerobics, for instance, and I go to Women in Banking and Finance events after work.'

Carole, 36, bank manager

'I have sacrificed less. I consider time at work to be time for myself. I have chosen to be there.'

Karen, 36, entertainments manager

'I feel so full of energy by being both part time: worker and mum.'

Angela, 38, part-time clerical officer

'It gets easier as the children get older. Normally it works smoothly, but at times one part of your life gets harder: my father is terminally ill with cancer and I'm a daughter as well!'

Lynn, 41, occupational therapist

'What I have sacrificed is not having enough time with Daniel after school. We do not get in until 6 pm, and it is a rush to do everything by bedtime. Otherwise, on balance, my working is a plus.'

Gillian, 48, accounts manager

'Sometimes I would like to be more of a home-maker, so maybe I bake at the weekend or paint with the children, only to find my neighbour, who is at home all day, does none of this with her children. She thinks I'm Superwoman.'

Kathleen, 36, human resources adviser

'No, the pressure comes not from the career but from my desires and from what I want from life. I want a certain standard of living, a certain kind of house, a certain lifestyle, a freedom from want (I had a childhood of poverty), a certain future for the children. And I feel I need to work in order to achieve these.'

Kwen, 35, psychologist

'Definitely sacrificed more, Sara will never be young again, and I have missed a lot of that. It doesn't matter what advantages there are, they can't compensate for that.'

Julie, 35, hand embroiderer

Do you ever feel guilty? If so, what about?

'I feel guilty if my house has not been hoovered from top to bottom twice a week. If my house is a mess, I am a mess and that upsets me.'
 Joy, 41, general assistant/business proprietor/care assistant

'I worry all the time that I am doing neither job (parenting/paid work) well, although I'm told the opposite.'
Jackie, 36, accounts clerk/estate agent

'Yes, I did feel guilty when I worked part time. I was not really satisfied with any task, whether at home or at work. Now my day at work is rewarding and I am less tired than when I worked 9.30 am to 3 pm, when I never seemed to be in the right place at the right time!'
Lynda, 41, marketing executive

'I think I do all right. Sometimes I feel guilty when Katy rings me to say goodnight. I feel I should be tucking her up in bed instead of blowing her a kiss down the phone.'
Irene, 42, hotelier

'No, I think I do both jobs well. I just look hellish sometimes.'
Lynne, 33, publisher/public relations consultant

'No. I'm much happier working part time. I feel I have the best of both worlds.'
Pauline, 31, paediatric endocrine nurse specialist

'I think I am a selfish person and I enjoy my four hours a day at work and my leisure time. I also work hard at home and have a clean and happy household. I spend enough time with the girls and I don't think they miss out on things – although I quite often have guilty feelings about not doing enough for them, and perhaps I should be a more dedicated mother.'

Susan, 37, WP operator/clerk

'I feel I've put a lot of pressure on my partner because I'm studying for a degree (although we discussed it beforehand) and I feel guilty about that.'

Lynne, 33, student

'Of course I feel guilty. Show me a woman who doesn't and I'll show you a slab of granite.'

Sharon, 33, design manager

'No, I don't really feel guilty. I'm a better mother for working. I love the company of my children and sometimes give thanks for how "normal" they are compared to many that I come across at school.'

Sue, 36, deputy head teacher

How do you cope with being pulled in all directions?

'Mostly I cope very well, but about twice a year I have "panic attacks".'

Lesley, 40, photographer/book-keeper

'I can't cope with too much chaos. The answer, I think, is to delegate. My husband is cooperative when it involves childcare.'

Judy, 37, lecturer/musician

'Perhaps having no partner means that I have sufficient mental energy to look after my child, myself, our home and also work full time.'

Judy, 39, customer service officer

'I enjoy being pulled in all directions because the time flies past. No two days are the same. It's challenging and interesting.'

Claire, 34, marketing consultant

'By being prepared to compromise, by not being a perfectionist, by learning to know what must be done now and what can wait.'

Catherine, 39, senior secretary

'By giving myself the right to do things for me. If I believe that, the rest of the family does. When I need time, it's accepted that I should take it.'

Jean, 44, senior probation officer

'I become resentful. I also get stressed and on those days I feel I'm always late.'

Pauline, 39, teacher

'I hate being pulled in all directions. You have to take time out to think about what is going on.'

Margaret, 23, part-time bank official/fitness instructor

'I ended up off sick for 10 weeks last summer with depression and emotional exhaustion.'

Heather, 31, specialist nurse (infection control)

'From time to time I scream and yell and have hysterics. Then I grit my teeth and get on with it.'

Francesca, 31, horse breeder/business partner

'As my husband looks after the children, I don't feel particularly "pulled". I know the children are receiving as good care as I could give.'

Rebecca, 30, district forester

'Generally, I am okay when I am being pulled in all directions, but when I have PMT, I can go to pieces. I do feel that I have no time for myself; even my knitting is for other people.'

Tracey, 27, nanny/nursery nurse

'Sometimes I cope brilliantly, but when things go really badly, I dissolve into tears, and lean heavily on my partner for emotional support.'

Charlotte, 33, doctor/senior registrar

'I have a good moan with my working friends. We help each other out, collecting children from clubs etc. and I delegate as much as possible. With careful planning, it's amazing how much you can achieve.'

Elspeth, 38, teacher

'I cope, but badly. I think this will be more of a problem when Ben is older and wants me at school plays etc..'

Tracey, 31, sensory analyst

'I'm not sure how I cope; it just sort of happens! I always accept offers of help and I employ someone to do my housework once a week; she's a godsend.'

Wendy, 30, senior computer analyst

'As long as my partner's pulling in the same direction, I can cope fine. It's when we're not supporting each other any more that something will have to give.'

Nichola, 26, home-buying adviser

'On a bad day I do feel guilty about doing neither job well: when the freezer's empty, the milk's off and my purse is empty! I'm learning mentally to compartmentalize things, and then only looking into one compartment at a time.'

Elizabeth, 38, care assistant/Project 2000 trainee

Do you have any role models for a balanced life?

'A friend with three children under four who works full time is my role model. She revels in the chaos and is pretty relaxed about life. I strive for her outlook!'

Gillian, 35, systems training designer

'My role model is Mary Robinson – President of Ireland: an extremely qualified career woman with a very happy family life.'

Moira, 36, business consultant/area manager,
Prince's Youth Business Trust

'My role models for a balanced life are my friends who work and have supportive husbands who share in the household/childcare areas. They seem to be the happiest.'

Patricia, 37, teaching assistant

'I don't have role models. Friends who were role models have surprised me with marriage break-ups etc..'

Clare, 42, PA/secretary

'My role model is my perfectly balanced best friend of 35 years' standing.'

Lindsay, 39, supply teacher

'One woman is an accountant who works three days in an office and sometimes at home. She has two children and a husband. She manages to swim and ride horses. Another woman has one child and a husband; she used to childmind for two school children and one nursery child. She also worked four nights in an office and has a student staying with the family.'

Elizabeth, 35, filing clerk

'My role model for a balanced life is my Auntie Julie. She started off in council accommodation, has worked extremely hard over the years and is now very comfortably off in a beautiful home. She has had several businesses as well as two children.'

Sarah, 26, florist/student

'I don't have role models. The rich and famous leave their kids with minders more than most.'

Janet, 39, catering assistant

Has anyone ever criticized you for being a working mother?

'Yes. One of our children is hyperactive and the school said that this could be because we're working parents and the child goes to a minder.'

Alison, 37, senior registrar (obstetrics & gynaecology)

'My second husband criticized me for not being like his mother. Yet he put me in the position where I had to work, by not being able to support us to the level I expected at that time.'

Charlotte, 50, probation officer

'My mother-in-law has criticized me: "It's amazing the price the young are prepared to pay for the privilege of not having to look after their own offspring."'

Rona, 28, researcher for Executive Search Agency

'Husband's grandmother, who thinks women these days are too quick to send their children to nurseries etc. so that they, selfishly, can work. She forgets that she had a nanny and did not even work.'

Nicola, 29, antique furniture restorer

'One person (a woman older than me with no children) actually told me that she didn't agree with working mums. I said if she paid my mortgage, I'd go home. 18 months later she had a baby and went straight back to work!'

Lynne, 33, student

'Yes, one of my husband's customers said she thought it was disgusting that I worked full time, but in the next breath said I ought to be like other tradesmen's wives and be his secretary!'

Sarah, 25, general manager of retail/mail-order leisurewear company

'My husband's business partner has criticized me. He and his wife have six children and his wife has never worked a day in her life; needless to say, she is one of the most boring women you could ever meet.'

Susan, 45, student/company director

'My grandmother criticizes, because in her day people stayed at home and looked after their children. I don't actually think this made them better mothers, as they sat the children at the bottom of the garden in their prams while they did their housework, baking etc. Due to so many labour-saving devices

and convenience foods today, I'm sure that all children, whether their mums work or not, get a lot more "quality time".'
Anne Marie, 31, part-time sales assistant

'Full-time mums criticize you for not taking your child swimming: is it that vital for an under-two?'
Helen, 27, agricultural consultant

'My sister says that 90 per cent of the world's violence is caused by working mothers. I am still trying to work that one out!'
Claire, 36, social worker

'Yes, people have criticized; people who think only a mother can give children what they need in a one-to-one relationship. As my husband says, "What about fathers' relationships with their children?"'
Julia, 35, patent analyst

'A friend criticized me when she visited my seven-year-old daughter in hospital and I was coming after work.'
Carol, 45, teacher

'I had a childminder who asked if she could adopt my child as I didn't appear to want him. Not true.'
Jayne, 38, estate agent

'Yes, an elderly neighbour said that my son would be traumatized by me being a working mother. He is an A-grade student and hopes to study Law at university.'
Toni, 39, NHS senior manager

Which do you dread more: weekends or Monday mornings?

'Mondays. I look forward to weekends, but sometimes my high expectations are not met and I get disappointed.'
Mary, 56, customer services manager

'Neither, my life is great!'
Sue, 35, training manager

'I dread weekends when my partner is working and I'm alone with the tantrum monster – our three-year-old daughter – for two days. But when he's here, I dread neither weekends nor Mondays.'
Sharon, 33, design manager

'Neither – I look forward to both. By the end of the week, I'm looking forward to my time with my family, but by Monday I'm worn out by being a mum!'
Susan, 27, insurance clerk

'Weekends – I have to cook more.'
Jenny, 50, caretaker/domestic engineer

'Monday. Getting up in a rush and trying to get Molly dressed at the same time as playing, showering, putting on make-up etc..'
Sarah, 28, regional administrative officer

'I don't dread either. I love weekends to spend with Emilie and then by Monday I'm pleased to be a businesswoman again.'
Kerry, 36, application support & training
for developing countries

'Weekends – because on a Sunday, when we've arranged to take the kids out for the day, the phone usually rings and it's one of my staff saying they are off sick. So I have to go to work instead, and it disappoints everybody.'

Caroline, 32, kennels and cattery proprietor

'Weekends. I don't feel it's fair to take work home and often want to.'

Genevieve, 39, NHS administrator

'I dread Monday mornings more. I often doubt my ability to do my job and have this lurking dread that some catastrophe will expose my shortcomings.'

Christine, 30, financial controller

'Weekends. You're supposed to go out and have fun and (a) I can't afford to; (b) babysitters are a problem; and (c) I like the routine the weekdays give me.'

Wendy, 46, teacher/now a journalist

'Monday mornings: there's too much organizing to do. I do two hours' "work" before I get to work.'

Maggie, 37, programming consultant

'I don't dread any day. They are all different, sometimes tiring and stressful, but mostly enjoyable and good fun, whether it's at work or with Evie.'

Helen, 27, business development consultant

How do you think your children feel/will feel about the way you've lived your life?

'My children are very happy as they have lots of friends and interests. They accept things, but would prefer to have their dad with us.'

Jean, 44, doctors' receptionist/typist

'My older boys have admitted that although they complain about me working, they appreciate my need to do so and respect the fact that it does make me a more interesting person. Jack and Joe have never known anything else.'

Jackie, 36, accounts clerk/estate agent

'I think they are thoroughly enjoying themselves and love telling people I'm at school and have homework to do.'

Lynne, 33, student

'My daughter says that she's not going to get married as she doesn't want children; she wants some peace. She has also said that if she has children, she's not going to go to work because it is too hard. I hope she'll look back and be happy with how things were.'

Di, 30, quality control supervisor

'They enjoy the challenge of moving (nine times in 12 years): the extra explorations, unusual houses, new friends they meet.'

Lindsay, 39, supply teacher

'I hope I will bring her up to know that I love her more than anything, but independent enough for her to do what she wants.'

Sarah, 25, general manager of retail/mail-order leisurewear company

'Fine. Anna loves nursery and there's no way she could go there if I didn't work.'

Sarah, 31, training manager

'Approving. I disapproved of my mother vegetating at home.'

Julie, 29, accountant

'I think Ben will think more of his father because he spends more time with him. I'm always "busy in the kitchen".'

Julie, 33, secretary

'She wishes she was older so that we could go out together in the evenings. She's proud that I work in a school.'

Patricia, 37, teaching assistant

'I hope my child realizes that I was only human and had shortcomings too. I hope that she will know that I did my best for her and that she will feel she was loved and cherished.'

Audrey, 41, admin supervisor

'My daughters talk about when they will go out to work (aged six and four). I believe they accept this as the way I live and I hope they are proud of me.'

Carole, 36, bank manager

'They wouldn't thank me for staying at home, but I expect they'll complain about me when they're teenagers – when you can't do anything right anyway.'

Sharon, 33, design manager

'I think, as they get older, they will appreciate the creative atmosphere they were growing up in: the interesting people they meet and places that they go to.'

Sarah, 37, college lecturer (Fashion Design)

'My 22-year-old daughter said that she hoped she'd be just like me when she's 50. I was enormously pleased and flattered.'

Elizabeth, 51, fine art journal editor

'My children will feel that I was definitely strange, but never boring.'

Toni, 39, NHS senior manager

'I hope they will admire me and realize that they too can cope without a man to support them.'

Christine, 42, resource manager (publications)

'They don't know any different, but my son is just beginning to say that he would rather stay at home than go to nursery.'

Arabella, 33, interior designer

'What a dull old stick mum was.'

Brenda, 43, office worker

'My children feel that I was a fool to stay with a constantly unfaithful hubby for so many years!'

Raye, 49, personal assistant

'When I think back to how I felt about my own parents, my single most important memory is not being able to talk to them, and it's the one I want most to overcome with my own daughter. I don't expect her to want to be my best friend, but I hope there's never anything that she feels she can't say to me.'

Sheila, 33, director/company secretary

'I think my son thinks I'm too soft with my husband – an understatement really! My husband criticizes me because he has to make his own dinner etc..'

Mary, 51, government press officer

'I hope they will have fond memories of a happy childhood, certain in our love for them.'

Samantha, 30, quantitative market researcher

'My 19-year-old daughter loved it when I had a "good job". She was proud of me. She thinks I've gone "mumsy" now. I'm not sure about the other two.'

Carol, 43, self-employed business administrator

'They may possibly wish that I had been at home more when they got in from school when they were younger, to help with homework.'

Jan, 43, hotel manager

How well organized are you? Have you ever forgotten to pick up your child or attend an important work meeting?

'My mind is like a filing cabinet. I am so organized, it's unreal: Christmas presents are wrapped in August. I have never forgotten to pick Lauren up.'

Emma, 28, law student

'I have occasionally been late to collect my eldest son from the bus stop, because of work, but he has always been understanding. I make it a point to attend all sports days and parents meetings, but not every event organized by the school – it just isn't possible.'

Jackie, 36, accounts clerk/estate agent

'I'm very organized. I have never forgotten anything major, but when I started back at work I did dream that I had forgotten to take Lori to the childminder and had left her in the crib. That was enough to make me write everything down so I wouldn't forget.'

Jane, 35, PR/marketing manager

'I'm usually very organized, but sometimes I find there's no clean school uniform, or socks.'

Judy, 39, customer service officer

'I haven't forgotten the children or missed meetings, but I did once drive into work so absorbed in thought that it was only after I had parked the car that I realized I still had a child in the back who hadn't been delivered to the childminder. She chirped up: "Am I coming with you today?"'

Judith, 36, chartered physiotherapist

'Very well organized; you have to be if you work shifts. I even do a weekly menu as a guide to meals and shopping needs.'

Joanna, 43, nurse (casualty department)

'In my last Annual Report, my boss described me as "frighteningly well organized".'

Tina, 37, civil servant

'I have occasional lapses, like taking the kids to school on a bank holiday.'

Angela, 31, fundraiser

'I've a good memory and haven't forgotten anything major, but I do all kinds of stupid minor things, such as putting four-star petrol in our diesel car, because I've a lot on my mind.'

Penny, 39, freelance journalist/editor

'*Even the most organized person can forget something. I had one mix-up when both my husband and I thought the other was collecting our daughter from the childminder. She was there until midnight. It was awful.*'

Janet, 39, commercial manager of professional football club

'*Yes. I have forgotten to pick up a child – not mine, but a neighbour's!*'

Lindsay, 39, supply teacher (former WRAF personnel officer)

Tips for an easier life

1. Put everything on a 0–10 scale of importance, then you'll only do the things that matter.

2. Share roles and responsibilities with your partner and then trust him to do his bit totally – without looking over his shoulder constantly, or doing it for him.

3. Make some preparations the night before: fill the car with petrol/make sandwiches/get clothes ready etc.

4. Get all the labour-saving devices you can afford, which you think might be useful. And get outside cleaning help.

5. Have a filing system that works.

6. Work out which school events etc. are likely to be attended by most mothers. Go to those and explain to your child that you will not be able to attend the others.

7. Have a large family diary and put everybody's appointments in it. Check it every day.

8. Try and think ahead by organizing menus/cooking food, buying birthday presents/blank cards well in advance.

9. Buy in bulk.

10. Don't over-commit your free time: night school, jewellery/book parties etc. need to be dumped. Don't over-commit your child's time either, with Brownies, swimming lessons etc.

11. Try multi-tasking. Make the dinner, put on washing and play with the kids simultaneously.

12. Get up half an hour before everyone else and have an early night every other night.

13. Ensure that you are communicating effectively with work, childminders, partners and children.

14. Set aside only one night a week to do extra work (if you have to do it at all).

15. A cordless phone and answerphone are essentials.

16. Get to know other working mums. Help each other by sharing childcare.

17. Plan meals a week in advance and shop for those meals.

18. Cook easy meals, such as stir fries and casseroles.

19. Try and do some housework during the week so that you can have time at weekends to do other things with the children.

20. If your children are old enough, get them to help.

21. Don't make too many promises, in case you cannot keep them.

So is it worth it?

Interviewing hundreds of women for this book has been both an enriching and a humbling experience. I have picked up so many hints and strategies for making life easier, and at the same time realized that I am still very new at this working mother 'game'.

The same may be said for most employers. While men, in the last 20 years, have gradually become more aware of the fact that childcare and household chores were made to be shared, in order to make working mothers' lives more manageable, many employers still make few provisions to do the same. Some businesses create a lot of part-time jobs, but pay such low hourly rates that single parents cannot afford to have a job and pay for childcare, because they are better off living on benefit. It seems to be up to the individual mother – or father – who wants to spend more time with his children, to negotiate job shares or flexible working arrangements.

If we working mothers need help, we should ask for it and not be made to feel embarrassed or inferior to other work colleagues. Remember, we bring a lot of commitment and experience to the workplace and often work through lunch hours and late into the evening at home in order to be able to rush away with a clear conscience and in time to pick up children – a fact little noticed or appreciated by the 'Oh she's not a valuable team member, she always leaves early' brigade.

Working with inspiring people on SHE, and meeting so many of the readers over the past few years, has made me appreciate how wonderfully hectic our lives become when we have children, and how no problem is insurmountable if we look at it, and then tackle it, clearly.

We may all have heard it before, but that makes it no less true, that bringing up children to be happy, loving, responsible and useful adults is the most responsible and important job that any of us could ever wish to do. It is our decision whether we tackle this role full time, part time or within a job-share arrangement, but as long as the end result is good then we have every right to feel proud.

Of course, we all have a personal wish list that would improve the quality of our lives. It goes without saying that it would be great to receive more help from the Government and all our employers, but in the meantime we need to speak up for what we believe in and, more importantly, we must not forget to give each other all the support we can.

Going by friends' experiences, I can see that I have countless more stages to go through and obstacles to stumble over as Natalie grows up. But even so, much as I love my cheeky little girl – and it frightens me sometimes when I realize just how much I do feel for her – I know one thing for sure: along with 61 per cent of the women who helped with this book, I could never become a full-time mum.

Whether we're 20-, 30- or 40-something when we become mothers is almost irrelevant these days; we all still ask ourselves at some stage whether it is worth it, as we run madly, and never empty-handed, from one area of our lives to another.

I sometimes lust after life before Natalie, as I am missing the long weekend lie-ins; that wonderful feeling of an unplanned day stretching ahead with enough money to do or buy whatever I liked; spontaneity in everything from deciding to rush out to see the latest Brad Pitt film or go to the first night of a play on the way home from work, to enjoying champagne and unabandoned sex in the afternoon, rather than trying to draw Dumbo for the fifth time in half an hour. But neither my husband, Chris, nor I would ever wish to go back to those days, because we know how blessed we are to have her. Yes, as all parents know and sickeningly never tire of telling those wavering on the edge of parenthood, the rewards really are incalculable. A tiny hand in yours or a heartfelt 'I love you' as a child flings herself onto your lap, or rushes to hug your legs like the tightest Egyptian mummy's bandage, makes all the tireless juggling of work and home commitments worth it – at any price.

What would make your life easier as a working mother?

'Children who washed, dressed and fed themselves!'
Karen, 35, video editor/student

'Being able to complete my book-keeping studies and become self-employed.'
Caroline, 35, manager of a take-away

'A secretary at home.'
Lesley, 41, publisher

'More support from my husband. Even though it is now an accepted part of modern society, I still believe that when a wife and mother goes out to work, she then has two jobs, while her husband/partner has one. How many men ever wonder,

in an important meeting, what the family is going to have for tea? Or dash out during a break to buy bread? And if he goes away, does he organize food/clothes etc. for his wife and children?'

Mary, 51, government press officer

'Having a good holiday every year.'

Cherrie, 49, principal of a ballet school

'If my ex-husband paid up the maintenance arrears that have accrued over the past six years – approximately £3,000 a year. I've received about £1,000 in total in that time!'

Lucy, 38, secretary/PA & research interviewer

'A magic wand.'

Annie, 42, NHS chief executive

'Cheaper or subsidized childcare. I do a 40-hour week and after nursery fees I contribute £55 into our account. If I was single what would the options be? It's criminal that I would be better off not working.'

Sarah, 25, general manager of retail/mail-order leisurewear company

'The only thing that would make our life easier as working parents would be the kids being able to drive. We have become permanent taxis, and living six miles from town on bus routes that are adequate during the day and non-existent at night adds an annoying complication to our life.'

Terry, 43, photographic goods wholesaler

'Men who undertake 50 per cent of household tasks automatically.'

Stephanie, 31, midwife

'A full-time housekeeper! Working close to home – I drive 45 minutes each way.'

Mary, 56, customer services manager

'I can't think of a thing which would make my life easier, or I would have found it, or done it by now.'

Sheila, 33, director/company secretary

'Having working mothers in senior positions, who would appreciate the demands on us. Where I work this is rare. This would also help fathers to share the responsibilities without feeling guilty. I have been a working mum for eight years and little has changed. Mothers have to earn a substantial wage to cover childcare costs or else rely on relatives and friends.'

Diane, 32, teacher

'Having eight days in the week: five for work, two for weekends and one for ME.'

Frances, 38, personal assistant

'Shorter school holidays.'

Janet, 39, catering assistant

'Employers who had a system to look after children during school holidays. It is about time that the Government did more to help mums who go out to work. I'm one of the lucky ones, but it must be extremely difficult for single mums. Summer camps would be a good idea.'

Susan, 37, WP operator/clerk

'A couple more hours in the day; to have my mother living very near – unlikely as she died when I was 21 – and a sandwich-making machine.'

Gay, 34, representative for children's publisher

'Nothing would make life easier; I think I've organized my work schedule to perfection now.'

Lynn, 41, occupational therapist

'Self-washing/feeding babies, so that I could simply play with them.'

Catherine, 28, branch administrator

Could you go back to being a full-time mother?

'No, I think all women need to spend time doing and thinking about things unrelated to children. I appreciate that some women may not think this way, but I feel that you are a person in your own right, not just somebody's mum.'

Jackie, 36, accounts clerk/estate agent

'If we win the Lottery perhaps. Yes, I could, especially when both boys are at school. I would like to do my own thing during school hours and be there for them when they come home.'

Judy, 37, lecturer/musician

'I couldn't go back to being a full-time mother. I value my independence and love being in the working environment. I love dressing smartly and would not make so much effort if I did not work.'

Gillian, 48, accounts manager

'No, I need to work. Looking back, my mother didn't and when we'd grown up, she had nothing.'

Pauline, 31, paediatric endocrine nurse specialist

'Most people don't really have a choice about whether they work or not. I enjoy the independence. Had I not worked then I would probably have found divorce etc. far more difficult to cope with – both emotionally and financially.'

Jenny, 27, systems analyst/IT manager

'Only if I had a baby to look after. I cannot understand how anyone could want to stay at home with school-age kids. In the future I think more and more women will be able to work flexibly to fit in better with their families.'

Jane, 25, housing officer

'Never. We would have little money to enjoy ourselves and our marriage would become stale because I would slowly become boring to my husband.'

Julie, 29, accountant

'I could go back to it as I was a full-time mum for five years, although, I must admit, I would miss my work and colleagues. My job is a real challenge and I never know what I'll be doing from one day to the next. Six years ago the North Yorkshire Police offered maternity leave; now they offer a *Career Break System*, whereby women can take up to six years off in order to have a family. Part-time work can also be arranged for qualified officers. Just by the break being made available, it allows women to return to work as and when they feel the time is right. It costs thousands of pounds to train a police constable throughout their initial two-year probationary period. Offering a career break protects their investment, because the women returning to work will only need minimal re-training. I "take my hat off" to the North Yorkshire Police and hope that some day many more employers will go the same way.'

Angela, 31, police officer

'No, I couldn't go back to being a full-time mother. I tried it for about six months; it was the hardest job I ever had.'

Janet, 32, legal accounts manager

'Yes, I'd quit tomorrow if we didn't need the money. Children grow up too fast while you're working.'

Linda, 35, diocesan registry clerk

'No, I couldn't go back to being a full-time mother. I lost lots of confidence and self-esteem while I was on maternity leave. I admire full-time mums and wish I could be satisfied with that, but I need more, and want to be a professional and use my skills.'

Kathleen, 36, human resources adviser

'No, because my son has his own life with his friends and grandparents, and I would be surplus, sitting around at home for two days a week.'

Lynda, 35, estate agent/hand model

'Yes, if circumstances demanded. I am sure I would find plenty to occupy me – in the community, for instance. I find that now my children are older, I can do more things with them. The first years of their lives are the most difficult in terms of boredom and pacing.'

Kwen, 35, psychologist

'No, I couldn't go back to being a full-time mother. I would be bored, and get fat and lazy.'

Jill, 40, sales coordinator

'No, full-time motherhood is harder than full-time paid employment. You can't resign and you have total responsibility.'

Andrea, 43, speech and language therapist/language teacher

Any other thoughts on being a working mother at the end of the twentieth century?

'*Male attitudes must change; men expect wives to take on a job, do the school runs, cook and clean etc. and still want sex at night. My ex-husband's attitude was: "Well, you wanted to go back to work, so you can fit it in with all the other jobs."*'

Raye, 49, PA

'*I think things are getting more difficult for working mothers rather than easier, because there is an office culture now that says it's not the quality of your work that matters, it's the hours that you put in that counts. If you leave on time, you're not seen as being committed to the organization. There is a huge drive within many organizations to reduce costs, so people are made redundant or not replaced and those that remain are expected to work harder and harder. This turns many people against returning to work after the birth of a first child. In many organizations good, skilled labour is in short supply. Where I work we need good, skilled nurses. So, I really feel that we have no choice. We have to be considerate to people's family needs and value people's lives outside work or we will continue to lose good people.*'

Annie, 42, NHS chief executive

'*Our children rely on us to care for them, whether in paid employment or not. No one is perfect, but provided we manage to care for them, and love them, and they know it, I cannot see that it makes one iota of difference whether women work or not. After all, many fathers are loved, needed, and play a part in family life while they work.*'

Margaret, 47, senior medical laboratory scientific officer

'The Government should do its duty and make available proper childcare facilities. Women are a vital part of our working community and should not have to choose between motherhood and careers.'

Susan, 27, insurance clerk

'When we can talk about working fathers, we'll be getting there. Families ought to be made on the premise that they are an economic unit and discussions on who does what should be clearly sorted before children appear on the scene.'

Jean, 44, senior probation officer

'I'm lucky to be living and working in France where facilities exist for working mothers. All children are treated the same and no woman feels "abnormal" or guilty.'

Kerry, 36, application support & training for developing countries

'For the past 10 years I've been writing articles saying that it's going to get easier, but actually I'm pessimistic. The United Kingdom lags behind Europe and employers are blinkered.'

Penny, 39, freelance journalist/editor

'Being a working mother is stressful and lonely. You realize that you are in a minority and sometimes wish that you had sufficient money to be able to give up for a year or so. Having said that, my children are wonderful and I often feel very sorry for the childless high-fliers.'

Kate, 30, charity manager

'I think we women need to accept that we are not the same as men. We have maternal feelings that result in guilt if we arrange our lives as men do. I hope future working mothers will realize this and organize their lives accordingly. A marriage partnership is a team life and we bring different talents into it. What we need is more recognition for a mother's talents, and acceptance of the fact that it is a valuable and worthwhile job. My husband loves his children, but he still trots off to the other side of the world to work – whereas I could never ever do that.'

Ann, 41, chartered accountant

'Women must get better wages. Earning a reasonable wage would make life easier. Most working mums are paid less than £5 per hour for responsible, demanding jobs. This is not a fair rate.'

Jean, 44, doctors' receptionist/typist

'I wonder if the women who fought so hard for emancipation and the vote would have dreamed that women would ultimately be accepted in society to do a "man's job" in the office, then come home and, wearing their "domestic engineer" hat, do another full-time job. The only thing we do seem to be able to control is the timing and frequency of our pregnancies (if we're lucky). Otherwise, I believe that women now may not be any better off than their Victorian counterparts.'

Jane, 33, local government manager

'The number of working mothers is on the increase. This is a good thing if it is because women do not want to waste their education/skills/training. I believe, however, that it is also due to the fact that people's material expectations are higher, and this is not a good thing.'

Victoria, 34, chartered accountant

'I love my children to bits and would die for them, but if I had my time again, I wouldn't bother having them. I do not feel that I am very maternal and the older they get the brighter the light at the end of the tunnel is getting. I can see unlimited freedom coming up and, quite frankly, I can't wait. I think I have done my bit and devoted years to my kids and an ungrateful ex-husband. It's my turn now!'

Joanna, 43, nurse

'By the end of the 20th century, I hope that I am still a hard-working wife and mother. I have fulfilled my role in setting up our new business and have new ambitions which I want to pursue. My dream is to write a book, so if I start now and find a few more hours in the day, I just might complete it.'

Francesca, 31, horse breeder/business partner

'Our job role has changed so much in society, but we are still expected to be a wife, mother and to work. I think the men are slowly coming round, however, to helping us in the house.'

Sue, 35, training manager

'There should be more job shares. More people should work fewer hours. Our whole employment set-up is wrong in this country. A few people are doing all the work and are overworked; many are out of work and would love to work. We need to share the work for the benefit of all men and women.'

Mary, 46, teacher

'I would say that any mother is a working mother, and if a woman wants to be with her children full time and can afford to, do that, it is her decision, and she deserves recognition for having a worthwhile occupation. On the other hand, if she wants to have a career outside the domestic environment, then that's fine too, and she should be given support, both by the Government (where have all the state nurseries and after-school clubs gone?) and by her friends and family. No one choice is more worthy than the other.'

Deborah, 36, freelance journalist

Useful Addresses

British Activity Holiday Association
22 Green Lane
Hersham
Walton on Thames KT12 5HD
Tel: 01932 252994

Sets standards for the activity holiday industry and provides a list of residential holidays and day centres for unaccompanied children aged four years and above.

British Association for Counselling
1 Regent Place
Rugby CV21 2PJ
Tel: 01788 578328

CACHE
(Council for Awards in Children's Care and Education)
8 Chequer Street
St Albans
Herts
Tel: 01727 847636

The awarding body which specializes in training and assessment for childcare, education and playwork. Awards inculde NVQs and the CACHE Diploma in Nursery Nursing (NNEB).

CRY-SIS
BM Cry-sis
London WC1N 3XX
Tel: 0171 404 5011

A telephone support line for parents with babies who cry excessively and sleep poorly.

Daycare Trust
Wesley House
4 Wild Court
London WC2B 4AU
Tel: 0171 405 5617

A national childcare charity which provides information and advice for parents, and works nationally for better childcare provision in the UK.

Equal Opportunities Commission
Overseas House
Quay Street
Manchester M3 3HN
Tel: 0161 833 9244

Established to fight descrimination and to promote equality between women and men.

Family Mediation (Scotland)
127 Rose Street South Lane
Edinburgh EH2 4BB
Tel: 0131 220 1610

Supports affiliated services throughout Scotland who work with separating and divorced parents to best meet the interests, and to protect the future of their children.

Family Mediation (Cardiff)
As above
33 Westgate Street
Cardiff
South Glamorgan CF1 1JE
Tel: 01222 229692

Gingerbread Association Advice Line
16 Clerkenwell Close
London EC1R 0AA
Tel: 0171 336 8184
e-mail: ginger@lonepar.demon.co.uk

For advice on all issues affecting lone parents.

Home Run
Cribau Mill
Llanvair Discoed
Chepstow
Gwent NP6 6RD
Tel: 01291 641222
e-mail: info@homerun.co.uk
Fax: 01291 641777

The leading magazine to help all those running their own businesses from home, or small offices.

Kids' Club Network
3 Muirfield Crescent
London E14 9SZ
Tel: 0171 512 2112

An organization that develops and promotes after-school care for children.

The Maternity Alliance
45 Beech Street
London EC2P 2LX
Tel: 0171 588 8582

Works to make life better for pregnant women, new parents and their babies. Also runs an advice line and produces a variety of leaflets for working mothers.

Meet-a-Mum Association
14 Willis Road
Croydon
Surrey CRO 2XX
Tel: 0181 665 0357

Offers friendship and support to new and expectant mothers, and extra support to those suffering post-natal illness.

Nannytax
PO Box 988
Brighton BN2 1BY
Tel: 01273 626256

The UK's leading payroll service for parents who employ a nanny. Brochure obtainable.

National Childbirth Trust
Alexandra House
Oldham Terrace
Acton
London W3 6NH
Tel: 0181 992 8637

A voluntary organization whose aim is to put parents in touch with other parents, and to provide support and help throughout pregnancy and childbirth.

National Childminding Association
8 Masons Hill
Bromley
Kent BR2 9EY
Tel: 0181 466 0200

A membership organization and registered charity which works to support childminders, parents and children, and to promote and encourage higher standards in daycare.

National Council for One-Parent Families
255 Kentish Town Road
London NW5 2LX
Tel: 0171 267 1361

Sends out information packs to one-parent families and provides useful addresses to help them.

National Family Mediation
9 Tavistock Place
London WC1H 9SN
Tel: 0171 383 5993

Provides a local contact for National Family Mediation services and offers help to separating or divorcing couples, to help them make joint decisions – particularly about arangements for their children.

New Ways To Work
309 Upper Street
London N1 2TY
Tel: 0171 226 4026

Provides information and advice on flexible working arrange-ments. Assists individuals by sending out basic information packs and offering a telephone hotline.

Parents At Work
5th Floor
45 Beech Street
Barbican
London EC2Y 8AD
Tel: 0171 628 3578

Campaigns on childcare, and provides information on childcare and employment rights for working parents.

Parents Anonymous for Distressed Parents
8 Manor Gardens
London N7
Tel: 0171 263 8918/0181 689 3136

A telephone helpline for parents under stress.

Pre-school Learning Alliance
69 King's Cross Road
London WC1X 9LL
Tel: 0171 833 0991
Childcare helpline: 0171 837 5513

The single largest organization providing quality education and care for the under-fives in Britain. It has 20,000 member pre-schools, attended by 800,000 children. The childcare line gives advice to parents looking for childcare provision.

Relate National Marriage Guidance
Herbert Gray College
Little Church Street
Rugby
Warwickshire CV21 3AP
Tel: 01788 573241

Provides services for couples in the making, sustaining and ending of intimate relationships, and also provides counselling and support for children when their families break up.

Relate (Northern Ireland)
76 Dublin Road
Belfast BT2 7HP
Tel: 01232 323454

Women Returners' Network
100 Park Village East
London NW1 3SR
Tel: 0171 468 2290

Seeks to facilitate the re-entry of women to education, training and employment. Provides a national information service for women seeking to return to work.